Job Interview Questions Series

JSP-SERVLET

INTERVIEW QUESTIONS
YOU'LL MOST LIKELY BE ASKEd

358
Interview Questions

JSP-Servlet

Interview Questions You'll Most Likely Be Asked

ISBN-10: 1-946383-10-4
ISBN-13: 978-1-946383-10-5

Library of Congress Control Number: 2016920127

Vibrant Publishers books are available at special quantity discount for sales promotions, or for use in corporate training programs. For more information please write to **bulkorders@vibrantpublishers.com**

Please email feedback / corrections (technical, grammatical or spelling) to **spellerrors@vibrantpublishers.com**

To access the complete catalogue of Vibrant Publishers, visit **www.vibrantpublishers.com**

Table of Contents

Dear Reader,

Thank you for purchasing **JSP-Servlet Interview Questions You'll Most Likely Be Asked.** We are committed to publishing books that are content-rich, concise and approachable enabling more readers to read and make the fullest use of them. We hope this book provides the most enriching learning experience as you prepare for your interview.

Should you have any questions or suggestions, feel free to email us at reachus@vibrantpublishers.com

Thanks again for your purchase. Good luck with your interview!

- Vibrant Publishers Team

facebook.com/vibrantpublishers

JSP-Servlet Interview Questions

Review these typical interview questions and think about how you would answer them. Read the answers listed; you will find best possible answers along with strategies and suggestions.

This page is intentionally left blank.

Chapter 1

Servlet

1: What is the difference between JSP and Java Servlet?

Answer:

JSP is a web scripting language that's embedded inside the HTML code for a page and is based on Java. Servlets are java programs that are written and compiled in a proper Java environment. You can write dynamic HTML content in Servlets. JSP is a view whereas Servlets are controllers. JSP ultimately compiles into a servlet before it runs and hence, is a little slower compared to the Servlets. JSP is preferred when there's very little server-side data manipulation required. If there's a lot of data manipulation involving complex business functions, the Servlets are preferred. JSP is easier to write as the scripting within the HTML code is easier to manage. With Javascript, JSP can easily manage client-side matters whereas the Servlets are purely server-side.

2: Explain the tasks of a Servlet.

Answer:

A Servlet's tasks include reading all implicit and explicit data sent by the client, process the requests at the server-side to generate results, and send this result as implicit or explicit to the client. Explicit input data would be form data as input or selected by the client. This is explicitly input or selected by the client to retrieve some information or to provide some information which has to be saved in the database. Implicit input data would be the request headers or other hidden elements such as status codes etc. which are set at the client's side while selecting some option. Explicit output would be the HTML displayed on the client's browser with the information requested. Implicit output would be the request headers and status codes sent by the server.

3: Explain Servlet Mapping.

Answer:

Servlet mapping is the method used to map the servlet classes and packages to a particular web application. It is done using the *<servlet-mapping/>* xml tag. The set of servlets and the classes defined in them are mentioned within the *<servlet-mapping/>* tags in the web.xml file. When the jsp page accesses a particular package or servlet class, the web.xml fetches this mapping and accesses the corresponding class file which has the servlet class definition. For example,

```
<servlet-mapping>
<servlet-name>healthdrinks</servlet-name>
<url-pattern>/health_drink/*</url-pattern>
```

</servlet-mapping>

Here, the <servlet-name/> contains the name of the servlet to be executed for the url patterns mentioned within the <url-pattern/> tags. The string mentioned within the url-pattern tag is case sensitive.

4: Explain what happens when a client requests a jsp page from the browser.

Answer:

When the client browser tries to access a particular jsp page, the corresponding jsp server is identified from the URL first. The jsp server checks for an existing compiled servlet corresponding to the requested page. If the page is not found or if the class is older than the latest jsp page, it has to be compiled first. The requested jsp page's java components are compiled into servlet and forwarded to the servlet engine which is a part of the web server. The Servlet engine loads the compiled servlet class and executes the same. The result is written as static HTML content and passed on to the web server as an HTTP response. It finally reaches the browser which displays the HTML content to the user.

5: Why do we need JSP when Servlets are there?

Answer:

Even when you are writing JSP code, you know that ultimately it is going to get converted into java code and a servlet. The jsp page's server-side scripts are compiled into java servlet class and that's what is executed. We can code a java servlet instead. But the main advantage of jsp pages is that they are much simpler to code and implement. The HTML tags will be a real pain to write using the java println statement. Instead, the required minimal scripts are included between the HTML tags, making the jsp pages easier to maintain. When using JSP, you can get the user interface coded separately and just include the required java elements within the scripting tags.

6: What is SSI (Server Side Includes)?

Answer:

Server side includes (SSI) are the directives and servlet code embedded within HTML pages to add some dynamically generated data retrieved from the server into the HTML pages.

```
<html>
<head> SSI </head>
<body>
<p> Username is
<servlet code=loginServlet>  // It will call loginServlet and return the output to html page
<param name=id value=123>
</servlet>
</body>
</html>
```

It will take the id from the HTML page and retrieve the username from the servlet file.

7: How do servlets handle multiple requests simultaneously?

Answer:

The Servlet container will create a single instance and multiple threads for a servlet. When multiple requests arrive simultaneously, the container synchronizes these requests by creating a new thread for each request and calls the service() method. The Service() method will be called for each request so as to handle these multiple requests.

8: What is the difference between GenericServlet and HttpServlet?

Answer:

The differences between GenericServlet and HttpServlet are:

a) HttpServlet is for the HTTP protocol requests and is protocol dependent. It is extended from GenericServlet and inherits all the properties of a GenericServlet.
b) GenericServlet is for all protocols such as FTP and is a protocol independent. It is sufficient to implement service() method to implement genericservlet. It implements the LOG method of ServletContext interface.

9: If we need to perform a login validation before hitting our application servlet, what could be done?

Answer:

To perform a login validation, we can use ServletFilter. This is mainly to provide authorization for all the pages given in the application. Only a single filter is needed to enable the authorization.

10: Who is responsible to create a servlet instance?

Answer:

Web container is responsible to create a servlet instance.

11: What is Servlet Collaboration?

Answer:

Servlet Collaboration refers to the communication between servlets. Information can be shared among the servlets through some method invocations, such as:

a) RequestDispatcher (forward() or include())
b) response.sendRedirect()
c) System.getProperties().put("name", "ABC") and String s1 = System.getProperty("name");
d) ServletContext

12: What is the architecture of a Servlet Interface?

Answer:

The architecture of a Servlet Interface is as given below:
Servlets >> GenericServlet >> HttpServlet >> CustomServlet
javax.servlet is the package which contains interfaces and classes.

13: What are the objects a servlet would receive during client interaction?

Answer:

A servlet would receive two objects during client interaction. They are:

a) ServletRequest interface
b) ServletRespose interface

14: Why do we not have constructors in servlets?

Answer:

The init() method is used for instantiating the servlets instead of constructors. The servlet container will take care of instantiating the servlet hence an explicit constructor is not required. Initialization code can be placed within init() method as we would have placed within the constructor. It will be called by the container once it has loaded the servlet at the first request.

15: How would you get the real path of the current servlet?

Answer:

We can retrieve the current servlet's real path using getRealPath() method:

System.out.println(request.getRealPath(request.getServletPath());

16: How would you call one servlet from another?

Answer:

A servlet can be called from another:

a) Using RequestDispatcher
b) Using URLConnection or HttpClient
c) Using response.sendRedirect

17: What are the different types of Servlets available?

Answer:

The different types of Servlets available are:

a) Generic Servlet
b) HttpServlet

18: Explain about HttpServlet and its methods.

Answer:

Httpservlet extends the GenericServlet class. A servlet class which implements HttpServlet class should override one of the below methods.

The methods of httpservlet are:

a) doGet()
b) doPost()
c) doPut()
d) doDelete()
e) getServletInfo()
f) service()

The service() method is not normally overridden since it dispatches the HTTP requests automatically to these appropriate methods. If service() method are to be overridden, doGet() or doPost() methods should also be invoked explicitly from the overridden service() method else super.service() method should be invoked from the overridden service() method to preserve the original service() method's functionality.

19: What are the advantages of Servlets?

Answer:

The advantages of Servlets are:

a) **Platform independent:** Once it is compiled, it can be run in any web server
b) **Threadsafe:** Different threads are created for different requests in a multithreaded environment

20: Name the servers available for deploying Servlets.

Answer:

The various servers available for deploying Servlets are:

a) Netscape
b) IBM Websphere
c) Oracle
d) Tomcat webserver
e) Apache
f) Weblogic

21: What would happen if I want to use the Servlet 2.1 API instead of Servlet2.0 API?

Answer:

If we use Servlet 2.1 API instead of Servlet2.0 API, servlet to servlet communication will not work as the communication using servletcontext methods like getServlet() and getServlets() have been deprecated. It will return null.

22: How would you avoid IllegalStateException in Servlet?

Answer:

IllegalStateException in Servlet happens when the servlet attempts to write into the response object (output stream) after it has been redirected or committed. It can be avoided using a return statement immediately after response.sendRedirect() or forward() methods. For example,

```
public void doGet(HttpServletRequestreq,
HttpServletResponseresp) throws ServletException, IOException {
    if(s1.equals(s2)) {
        response.sendRedirect("login.jsp");
        return;
```

```
    }
}
```

23: How would you make servlet stop timing-out when processing a long database query?

Answer:

If the database query takes several minutes to execute, the browser will time out before it retrieves the result for that request. To avoid this, we can use Client-pull/client-refresh/server polling, which makes the client to automatically refresh after a predetermined period of time. In this case, the client will poll the servlet in a regular period of time to fetch the page, which will make the servlet check the response object value and refetch the details. It would be able to send "Please wait while processing the request ..." message to the client browser until the request gets processed.

<META http-equiv="Refresh" content="15; url="welcome.html" />

24: Why is HttpServlet declared as abstract even though it has concrete methods?

Answer:

HttpServlet contains methods such as doGet(), doPost(), doPut(). Since it is declared as abstract, it does not require all of its methods to be implemented. We can implement the methods based on the HTTP request or requirement. Otherwise we must implement all the methods including those which are not required.

25: How would you refresh a servlet automatically if any data gets updated into database?

Answer:

Servlet can be refreshed using client side refresh or server push if any data gets updated into database.

26: Describe the difference between URL encoding and URL rewriting.

Answer:

The difference between URL encoding and URL rewriting are:

a) **URL encoding:** Transforms user input into CGI form which will trim spaces and punctuation, replacing them with special characters. URL decoding is a reverse process of encoding which will transform CGI format back to normal format. We use encode() and decode() methods of java.net.URLEncoder and java.net.URLDecoder classes. E.g. Input >> "We're #1!" and Transform Into >> "We%27re+%231%21"

b) **URL rewriting:** Additional information such as session id or parameters are appended at the end of the URL. E.g. http://localhost:8080/Demo/servlets?param1=abc

27: What is the use of Servlet Wrapper classes?

Answer:

Servlet wrapper classes are ServletRequestWrapper and ServletResponseWrapper. The subclasses are HttpServletRequestWrapper and HttpServletResponseWrapper classes. It uses wrapper or decorator design pattern. It provides custom implementation of subclasses which extends servletrequest and servletresponse types. The methods are invoked through the wrapped request or response objects.

28: What is servlet chaining?

Answer:

Servlet chaining is a mechanism where the output of one servlet will be sent to a second servlet and the output of second servlet will be sent to a third servlet. The output of the last servlet will be sent to web browser/container.

29: What are the functions of Servlet Container?

Answer:

The functions of Servlet Container are:

a) **JSP support:** Converts JSP page into servlet class, for example, Login.jsp will be converted to Login_jsp.java
b) **Multithreading support:** Creates separate threads for each request and calls service()
c) **Communication support:** Handles communication between web server and servlets
d) **Declarative security:** Maintains security in web.xml using authentication techniques
e) **Lifecycle management:** Manages servlet lifecycle such as loading, instantiating, service, and destroys servlets which are eligible for garbage collection

30: What is Server Side push and what is it used for?

Answer:

If the client requests data from the server, it is called Client pull. i.e. the client pulls the data from the server. Sometimes the server needs to continuously send data to the client to maintain sync between server database and client page. This is called Server side push. For instance, monitors which display online status such as airport and share market status.
Server keeps sending the data; client receives it and waits for the next information. The server does not create a new TCP connection for each request. It leaves the connection open after sending the initial data to the client. This is an expensive implementation, as the sockets remain open.

31: What is Client refresh/Client pull mechanism and how do we achieve it?

Answer:

Since server side push is an expensive approach, we can use the client refresh mechanism. It will automatically refresh the client browser page every 3 or 5 seconds (given below).Every 3 seconds the client will send a request to the server for the information and servlet will retrieve and send it to the browser. HTTP-EQUIV attribute information will be added to the http response header.
<META HTTP-EQUIV="Refresh" CONTENT="3;
URL=/servlets/testServlet/">

32: How would you achieve/make Client Auto Refresh using servlets?

Answer:

Client browser page will be refreshed every 5 (given) seconds. i.e server will send request to client every 5 seconds using addHeader() method of response object till the servlet gets destroyed.

```
public void doGet(HttpServletRequest req,
HttpServletResponseresponse) throws ServletException,
java.io.IOException {
    HttpSession session = req.getSession();
    response.addHeader("Refresh", "5");
    response.setContentType("text/html"); //If response is text
    message
}
```

33: What types of protocols are supported by HttpServlet?

Answer:

Httpservlet extends GenericServlet class and supports Http and Https protocols whereas GenericServlet supports various protocols.

34: How would you send data from servlet to Javascript?

Answer:

Data from servlet can be sent to Javascript as below:

```
publicvoiddoGet(HttpServletRequest request,
HttpServletResponseresponse)
throwsIOException,ServletException{
    PrintWriter out=response.getWriter();
    out.println("<script>");
    out.println("varuname='"+uName+"';");
    out.println("alert(uname)");
    out.println("</script>");
    }
```

```
}
```

35: How would you retrieve the name and version number of servlet or JSP engine?

Answer:

The name and version number of JSP engine or servlet is retrieved as below:

a) In servlet:

```
String info=
getServletConfig().getServletContext().getServerInfo();
```

b) In JSP:

```
//About application server
<%= application.getServerInfo() %>
// About JSP engine
<%=JspFactory.getDefaultFactory().getEngineInfo()getSpecificationVersion()%>
```

36: What is meant by parsequerystring?

Answer:

Parsequerystring parses the string in the form of a key and value pair similar to 'hashtable'. It appends the string with the URL. The query string will be generated if doGet() method is used and it will not be appended if doPost() method is used.

37: Which one is better to write binary data: JSP or servlet?

Answer:

Servlet is the best solution for writing binary data using ServletOutputStream. JSP is not suitable. The JspWriter class does not support writing bytes, it is designed to send text data and the

JSP container includes whitespaces, which are unnecessary when writing binary data.

Chapter 2

Servlet Lifecycle

38: You have a counter to know how many times your webpage was accessed. Where will you initialize it and where will you increment the counter? Explain.

Answer:

Declare and initialize it in the servlet class. Increment its value in the service () method. This is because the servlet is initialized only once when the web service is initialized. The service() method is called every time a new user accesses the webpage. If you want to make it persistent, write it into file inside the web folder or the database and access its value when the servlet is loaded. Another option to make it persistent is to use the database. Create a table with a single column for the counter. Once loaded, you can read and increment the value and overwrite its value in the file or the database before the servlet is destroyed.

39: Explain what happens during the initialization stage of a servlet.

Answer:

When the servlet is initialized, the init () method is called. It is called only once when the servlet server is initialized first time and not upon each request. All start-up tasks for the servlet application such as database connections, initializations etc. are defined in the init() method. It declares, defines and initializes the common application variables and objects. The server creates an instance of the servlet and immediately calls the init () method. Remember that only one instance of the servlet is created in a web application. The init () method will be called before the first service request from the client.

40: How do you pass hidden values from the form to the server?

Answer:

You can use the form post to pass the hidden form fields on submit. When you use the doGet() method, you have to pass on all parameter values to the server through the URL. This does not provide any privacy or security. But when you use doPost(), you can use the hidden fields in the form to pass on any secret value to the server. You can store the value in a hidden form field and access it in the servlet or jsp code. Hidden fields in a form cannot be seen by the user but can be accessed at the server side from the posted form variables. Even though the field is hidden, it will be best practice to validate the values and then perform any business logic since hackers can always find a way to manipulate the forms easily.

41: You request a servlet and it fails midway, what happens to initialized objects, variables and loaded classes?

Answer:

If the servlet fails during initialization itself, none of the memory allocations are completed. The servlet's init() method throws ServletException if it fails. When init() fails and the ServletException is raised. You can catch this exception and manually run a garbage collection. The destroy() method is automatically called by the server only when the entire web application fails and at this point, the destroy() method does garbage collection. If you have written some specific code such as database open in the servlet's init(), and the init() fails, the database connection is automatically closed and destroyed from the memory. But when you have multiple servlets running, it is best to call each one's init() within a try catch and handle the exception manually.

42: Can we replace the servlet init() method with a constructor?

Answer:

Although, you can define constructors for a servlet, it is not recommended as only one instance is created for a servlet. We cannot replace the servlet init() method with a constructor because, the servlet server calls the init() method automatically when it is requested and not yet loaded. The servlet server cannot dynamically call every constructor which will have a user-defined name as coded in the servlet. Instead, the init() method is called which can be overridden by each servlet. Moreover, we cannot pass the ServletConfig object to the servlet constructor for initialization. Another reason for the servlet not having constructor is that interfaces cannot have constructors.

43: If 10 users access a login page of your application at the same time, how many servlet instances will be created?

Answer:

It would create only a single servlet instance and it will be shared among all the requests. The Servlet container will handle multiple requests by generating multiple threads.

44: Which are the Servlet lifecycle methods?

Answer:

The servlet lifecycle methods are:

a) **init():** public void init(ServletConfigconfig) throws ServletException
b) **service():** public void service(ServletRequestreq, ServletResponse res) throws ServletException, java.io.IOException
c) **destroy():** public void destroy()

45: Can we override Servlet lifecycle methods? Is it a good practice?

Answer:

Yes, we can override lifecycle methods. However, it is not a good practice to override service() method since it would call other methods such as doGet() and doPost() implicitly depending on the type of HTTP requests. Therefore, if we override this method, we need to explicitly call these doXxx() methods depending on the requests.

46: Describe the Servlet Lifecycle.

Answer:

The various stages of servlet lifecycle are as follows:

a) **Initialization**: The servlets run within a servlet container. The servlet container will create a servlet instance and will execute init() method which would be called only once in its lifecycle. It will not be called for every request. Servlet will be created for the first time when the user invokes a URL corresponding to the servlet. It can be created when the server gets started using <load-on-startup>
b) **Execution**: For each client request of the servlet, the service() method will be called. This will in turn call the doGet() or doXxx() methods. In order to generate a response the doGet() or doPost() method will be called according to the requests
c) **Destruction**: It is invoked when servlet is removed from the container and eventually garbage collected. It contains code to release resources like JDBCconnection, which needs to be garbage collected

Servlet.class >> Instantiation (new) >> Initialization (init()) >> Execution (service()) >> doXxx() >> Destruction(destroy()) >> Garbage collection (finalize())

47: When would servlet-lifecycle method init() be called? (or) When would the servlet container create an instance for the servlet?

Answer:

The servlet-lifecycle method init() will be called (or) The servlet container will create an instance for the servlet :

a) Through the 'load-on-startup' tag given in the web.xml. It will make the servlet container preload the servlet and initialize when the server starts. The 'load-on-startup' tag should be set to a non-zero value

```
<servlet>
    <servlet-name>servlet1</servlet-name>
    <servlet-class>com.java.servlet.TestServlet</servlet-
    class>
    <load-on-startup>1</load-on-startup>
</servlet>
```

b) If the Servlet is not preloaded, the container will create an instance of the servlet once the first request is received. It will be called before the service() method is invoked

c) The initialization of the servlet can be requested directly by Server administrator

48: Can you get database connection using the servlet init() method?

Answer:

Yes. Since init() and destroy() methods are called only once for the servlet, we can handle database connection with these methods and use it for multiple requests. However, it is a good practice to get the reference of DriverManager and Datasource with the init() method, and get a connection for every request within the try-catch block. This ensures that if any exception occurs, the connection is always closed.

```
public void init(ServletConfigconfig) throws ServletException {
super.init(config);
try {
databaseUrl = getInitParameter("dbUrl");
    conn = DriverManager.getConnection(dbUrl, username,
    password);
    } catch(Exception e) {
        throw new UnavailableException (this,"Could not open a
        connection to the DB");
    }
}
(or)
InitialContextic = newInitialContext();
DataSource ds = (DataSource)ic.lookup("java:jdbc/TestDS");
(AND)
try {
    Connection con= ds.getConnection();
}catch(Exception e) {}
```

49: What is the difference between doGet() and doPost() methods?

Answer:

The differences between doGet() and doPost() are discussed below:

a) **doGet():**
   i) Parameters are appended with the URL as Query String with header information while sending data to the server and is visible to clients
   ii) Not secure

   iii) Only Limited amount of data can be sent to the server since the data would be sent in the HTTPrequest header
   iv) Maximum size of the data that can be sent is 240 bytes
   v) Used to retrieve data from the server
   vi) Can be bookmarked since query string is appended

b) **doPost():**
   i) Parameters will not be appended with the URL, they are sent in a separate line in the body of the HTTPrequest
   ii) Secure
   iii) No size limit
   iv) Used to send information to the server

50: How would you use both doGet() and doPost() methods for the same servlet?

Answer:

You can write doGet() method within doPost()method as this enables doPost() to delegate the control to doGet().

```
public void doPost(HttpServletRequestreq,
HttpServletResponseresp)
throws IOException,ServletException {
doGet(req, resp);
}
public void doGet(HttpServletRequestreq,
HttpServletResponseresp)
throws IOException,ServletException {
}
```

51: Why must we call super.init(config) method inside the init() method of a servlet?

Answer:

We must call super.init(config) method inside the init() method of a servlet because:

a) Servlet passes the ServletConfig object within the init() method but not in other methods
b) So if servlet requires access to the ServletConfig object outside the init() method then it would not be available
c) If super.init(config) method is called, it will call GenericServlet's init() method which has the implementation to store the ServletConfig object for future use
d) ServletConfig object information can be retrieved using getServletConfig() method

```
public void init(ServletConfigconfig) throws
ServletException {
super.init(config);
}
```

52: What would happen if a servlet does not call super.init(config) method within its init() method?

Answer:

Any call to the GenericServet's implementation using getInitParameter() or any call to the ServletConfig methods without super.init(config) method call will throw NullPointerException. So every servlet must call super.init(config)method before calling getInitParameter() or servletconfig methods. If a servlet implements javax.servlet.Servletinterface directly, then super.init() method is not needed.

53: Can we overload servlet's destroy method()?

Answer:

Yes, we can overload any java method. destroy() method/all servlet's lifecycle methods will be called by the servlet container. An overloaded method will not be called by the container and it will expect no-argument method. So if destroy() method contains arguments/different signatures, then it would not cause any problem.

```
public void destroy (String s1) {
}
```

54: Can we call destroy() method from init() method of a servlet?

Answer:

Yes. If init() method does not throw any exception then it will not stop/affect servlet's lifecycle. The container will continue to call service() method. However, if init() method throws an exception, then we can use this approach, for instance to call destroy() method to stop calling service() method to be called further. We do need to call ServletException to ensure that the service() method is not called.

55: If we call destroy()method of servlet will it be killed?

Answer:

The destroy() method will not kill the servlet. It will be called by the container to take the servlet out of service. All the resources, which it may be holding, will be stored/released. It can have other statements so as to tell what needs to be done before it takes the servlet out of service.

56: How would you avoid opening the database connection separately/multiple times by each servlet and initialize this connection before all the servlets access it?

Answer:

Opening the database connection separately/multiple times by each servlet can be avoided by the following steps:

a) Write a base/main servlet which extends HttpServlet class
b) Override init() method and create a database connection within this init() method
c) All remaining servlets need to extend this base servlet and access this connection
d) This base servlet will be called multiple times since all the sub classes that extend this base servlet need to be initialized and go through its lifecycle

This page is intentionally left blank.

Chapter 3

Servlet Reloading / Loading

57: I want my servlet program to reload the page whenever there's a change in some values. How do I get it done?

Answer:

Using the method setIntHeader() of the response object, we can make the servlet refresh or reload. The setIntHeader(String hdr, Int hdrVal) takes in the header name and the time interval in seconds in which you want to refresh the page automatically. So if you want to refresh your page automatically every 15 seconds, call *setIntHeader("Refresh", 15);* from your response object. Another method is to add a meta tag to the HTML asking the browser to refresh every set interval. You have to set the *http-equiv* attribute of the meta tag to *"Refresh"* and the *content* attribute to *"15"*. In fact, here you can even suggest moving to another page after 15 seconds if you make content = "15; url=http://www.yahoo.com"/>. Yet another method is to use the addHeader() method of

HttpServletResponse object which works similar to the setIntHeader() method of the Response object.

58: What are the occasions when the serlvet is reloaded automatically?

Answer:

The server is reloaded automatically when the servlet class is changed and when the database has new values. If you are using Tomcat4 or above as the server, it automatically detects any change in the servlet class definition from the time the servlet was last loaded and the current request, and reloads if any later version of the class is detected. Similarly, when the reloadable attribute of the database context and loader tags in server.xml are set to true, it automatically reloads the servlet when there is any change in the database.

59: Explain when a servlet is loaded.

Answer:

The servlet is loaded when there's a request. But you can set the load-on-startup parameter in the server.xml file to speed up or delay the loading of a servlet. If you have many servlets and do not want all of them to load during the startup which will delay the servlet startup process, you can set the value for load-on-startup to a higher number. If you have 3 servlets to load, the following code snippet will explain how the servlet loading priority is set:

```
<servlet servlet-name="Servlet_A" servlet-
class="<servlet_class_name>">
  <load-on-startup>45</load-on-startup>
```

```
</servlet>
<servlet servlet-name="Servlet_B" servlet-
class="<servlet_class_name>">
  <load-on-startup>10</load-on-startup>
</servlet>
<servlet servlet-name="Servlet_C" servlet-
class="<servlet_class_name>">
  <load-on-startup>23</load-on-startup>
</servlet>
```

Here the Servlet_B will be loaded first, since the load-on-startup value is set to 10 which is the lowest of the 3. The next to load will be Servlet_C with the second highest value of load-on-startup. The last one to load will be Servlet_A which has the highest value of load-on-startup.

60: Explain when and how the servlet unloads.

Answer:

The servlet usually unloads only when the web application is shut down or when the admin manually unloads the servlet. The destroy() method is usually not explicitly called because of a lot of reasons. Another instance when the servlet unloads is when the web server restarts. Then the servlet unloads first and then reloads either as soon as the server is up based on the loan-on-startup tag value defined in server.xml or when the first request is made.

61: My servlet is accessed by 5 people at the same time. What happens to the servlet processes running when one of their options call for a destroy()?

Answer:

The servlet waits for the currently running threads or processes to complete or release and after that only calls the destroy() method. The destroy() method closes the web application after running a thorough garbage collection, releasing all objects and memory elements and closing all open connections. But when one particular servlet forces the destroy() method to be called, while some others are still running, the server waits till all the currently running threads are completed. Then only it executes the destroy() method. In the mean while, you can access the event listener for the servlet and write all the important objects that need to be persistent into a database or file system.

62: What is Servlet Reloading?

Answer:

Servlet Reloading is:

a) Servers reload the servlets which have been put in the default servlet directory (server_root/servlets) automatically whenever the servlet class file is changed
b) ClassLoader objects (Primordial Class loader) are designed to load the class only once
c) Servers use a Custom class loader to load the servlets from its default directory
d) Servlet Reloading will not happen to the servlets which are found in server's classpath(server_root/classes)
e) Best practice to improve performance
    i) **During development:** Place servlets in default servlet directory
    ii) **During deployment:** Place servlets in server's

classpath

63: What will happen if a servlet is not loaded into the memory but the client had requested that servlet?

Answer:

When the client request comes in for a particular servlet and it is not loaded into memory, the servlet container will load and instantiate the servlet and process the request. Hence, there will be a time delay to process the first request of a servlet, but it will be faster for all subsequent requests.

64: What is lazy loading in servlet?

Answer:

Lazy loading in a servlet is when the servlet container will not load/initialize the servlet by default, when the server is started. It will load/initialize the servlet when it receives a request for that servlet for the first time.

65: Is there any way to unload a servlet from a web server memory without restarting the server?

Answer:

No. If the servlet needs to be unloaded from the server, it has to be removed from the application and the WAR file needs to be replaced. Some servers, such as JWS, contain admin modules that will load and unload servlets.

66: What is the reason of disabling auto reloading feature in production environment?

Answer:

Most JSP engine/application servers will reload the JSP's servlets dynamically. No need to restart the server whenever there is a change in JSP content, the application server will load it every time we configure that JSP's servlet. E.g. If you configure it for 5 seconds, it will reload the JSP's servlet for every 5 seconds.
This is useful during development as it avoids restarting the server after every JSP change. However, it will create poor performance in a production environment due to unnecessary loading on the class loader. Therefore, the auto-reloading feature should be disabled in the configuration file to improve performance

Chapter 4

Servlet Context

67: How do you add web components in Servlet 3 dynamically?

Answer:

Using the ServletContext from the ServletConfig object which is passed as a parameter to the init() method, you can add web components dynamically to the serlvet. The ServletConfig object passed along with the init contains a ServletContext object which has addServlet(), addListener(), and addFilter() methods. The addServlet() method lets you dynamically add a servlet to the ServletContext. Once you add the servlet, you can add its servlet mapping with addMapping() method.

ServletRegistration.Dynamic addDynServlet = ServletContextObj.addServlet (<new_Servlet_name>, <new_servlet_class>);

addDynServlet.addMapping(<url_patterns>); // As a string array

addDynServlet.setInitParameters(<init_parameters>); // As a

Hashmap

Similarly, you can add filters dynamically with addFilter() method and listeners dynamically with addListener() method of ServletContext.

68: Differentiate between Servlet Context and Page Context.

Answer:

ServletContext corresponds to a web application. There's only one ServletContext for a web application. PageContext corresponds to a page request. For each page request, a corresponding PageContext will be there. ServletContext is an interface whereas PageContext is an abstract class which contains complete information about the page. PageContext contains namespaces and key-value pairs of the attributes of the page and the implementation details. The ServletContext contains the details about the container that runs the jsp or the Servlet. PageContext will contain the information regarding the url request.

69: What are the uses of ServletContext?

Answer:

The ServletContext object contains the information about the container that calls the Servlet and the initial parameters passed for initiating the servlet. The ServletContext interface contains a lot of methods to access information about the runtime environment of the servlet and for interacting with other web components of the application. It also contains methods to create dynamic web components such as Servlets, Filters and Listeners. The ServletContext lets you retrieve and set configuration information in web.xml. It also allows communication between related web applications.

70: When is a servlet listener preferred over servlet context?

Answer:

When you are dealing with web applications with multiple entry points, servlet listeners are preferred over servlet context. One main reason for this is that an application can have only one ServletContext which contains the initial parameters when the application starts up. But when you have multiple entry points, you may need to repeat a lot of initialization code which is not possible using the ServletContext. Moreover, the ServletContext comes of use only when the first user requests the servlet. Until then, if there's some issue with the web components, we may not know. But the ServletListeners keep track of different events and lets you handle the events efficiently. For example, initialization is an event, destruction is an event, client request is an event, each session's beginning and ending are events modification of attributes are events etc. They provide more flexibility in handling events, particularly when it comes to web applications with multiple entry / exit points.

71: Can I access the ServletContext in one servlet from another servlet? Explain.

Answer:

Yes. The ServletContext lets you access the information regarding other web components including servlets in an application. In fact, it even lets you communicate with other web applications. You can also set the attribute values of other servlets provided you have the authority to do so. Using the getAttribute() method of ServletContext, you can access the value of the attribute. Similarly, using the setAttribute() method of ServletContext, you can modify or set the value of the attribute. Another option is using the RequestDispatcher object's methods.

72: What is the difference between <context-param> and <init-param> given in web.xml?

Answer:

The difference between <context-param> and <init-param> given in web.xml is:

a) **<context-param>:** These are context parameters available to the entire scope of the web application

```
<context-param>
<description>Context parameter</description>
<param-name>param1</param-name>
<param-value>paramValue1</param-value>
</context-param>
public void init(ServletConfigconfig) throws
ServletException {
    String param1 =
    config.getServletContext().getInitParameter("param1");
}
(or)
protected void doGet(HttpServletRequestreq,
HttpServletResponseresp)
        throwsServletException, IOException {
```

```
    String param1 =
    this.getServletContext().getInitParameter("param1");
}
```

b) **<init-param>:** These are init parameters available in the context of a servlet or filter in the web application

```
<servlet>
<servlet-name>servlet1</servlet-name>
<servlet-class>com.java.servlet</servlet-class>
<init-param>
<description> Init parameter </description>
<param-name> param2</param-name>
<param-value> paramValue2</param-value>
</init-param>
</servlet>
String param2=
getServletConfig().getInitParameter("param2");
```

73: What is the difference between ServletConfig and ServletContext interfaces?

Answer:

The difference between ServletConfig and ServletContext is as follows:

a) ServletConfig is used to initialize a single servlet using init() method and is implemented by the servlet container. The initialization parameters can be passed to the servlet using <init-param> tag in web.xml deployment descriptor. It is created per Servlet and is used to pass deployment time information to the servlet

```
public void init(ServletConfigconfig) throws
ServletException {}
    <servlet>
    <servlet-name>servlet1</servlet-name>
    <servlet-class>com.java.servlet</servlet-class>
    <init-param>
    <param-name>dbusername</param-name>
        <param-value>test</param-value>
    </init-param>
    </servlet>
    (AND)
    getServletConfig().getInitParameter("dbusername");
```

b) ServletContext is implemented by servlet container and is used for all the servlets available in the application within a single JVM to communicate with the servlet container. It is like an application global variable which can be shared among all the servlets in a web application deployed in a single JVM. The context parameters can be passed using <context-param> tag. ServletContext is contained within the ServletConfig and can be invoked using the ServletConfig object within a servlet

```
<context-param>
<param-name>dbpwd</param-name>
<param-value>root</param-value>
</context-param>
(AND)
ServletContext context =
getServletConfig().getServletContext();
```

74: When is the ServletContext object created?

Answer:

The ServletContext object is created in the following scenarios:

a) Servlet Container loads the servlet (Servlet.class) and invokes the default constructor (i.e. instantiate the Servlet) and init() method for initialization
b) Before invoking init() method it creates 2 objects: ServletConfig and ServletContext
c) If init-param(for servlet config - per servlet) is in web.xml then it creates an object containing these parameters and is passed to servletConfig object
d) If context-param is given in web.xml, it maps this data to ServetContext object. This data is shared by all the servlets in the application. E.g. database URL, username, password

75: What is ServletContext object?

Answer:

ServletContext object is used to store information that can be shared among all the servlets in an application. Each web application in a container will have a single servletcontext instance. It will be passed during servlet instantiation through init() method.

76: How many contexts will be created if five applications are running in a web container?

Answer:

One context will be created per application. Five contexts will be created for five applications.

77: Can we access ServletContext parameters in the JSP page and how would you retrieve it?

Answer:

Yes, we can access ServletContext parameters in the JSP page. It can be retrieved as shown below:

```
<%
getServletContext().getInitParameter("dbusername");
%>
```

78: How would you make a ServletContext object thread safe?

Answer:

ServletContext should be synchronized; this will ensure it will be thread-safe .Eg:

```
synchronized (getServletContext ()) {
}
```

79: How do you retrieve the servlet context?

Answer:

Servlet config contains the reference of servlet context. This context object can be retrieved using the getServletConfig.getServletContext() and this.getServletContext() methods.

80: What is the use of servletcontext method and getResourceAsStream()?

Answer:

The uses of servletcontext method and getResourceAsStream() are:

servletcontext method: Used to pass the resources/configuration file to the servlet when the configuration file's path is not defined in <init-param> of web.xml.

a) **getResourceAsStream():** Used to retrieve the resource/file from any location to servlet without using the class loader. It is better to place this file under WEB-INF to prevent it from being accessed by the browser directly.

```
InputStream is =
getServletContext().getResourceAsStream("/test.cfg");
```

81: How do you avoid hard coding the database name and driver details in all the servlets?

Answer:

Hard coding the database name and driver details in all the servlets can be avoided by:

a) Defining the database name and other details in the <context-param> tags in web.xml
b) Retrieving this database name in each servlet using getServletContext().getInitParameter() within init() method of the servlet

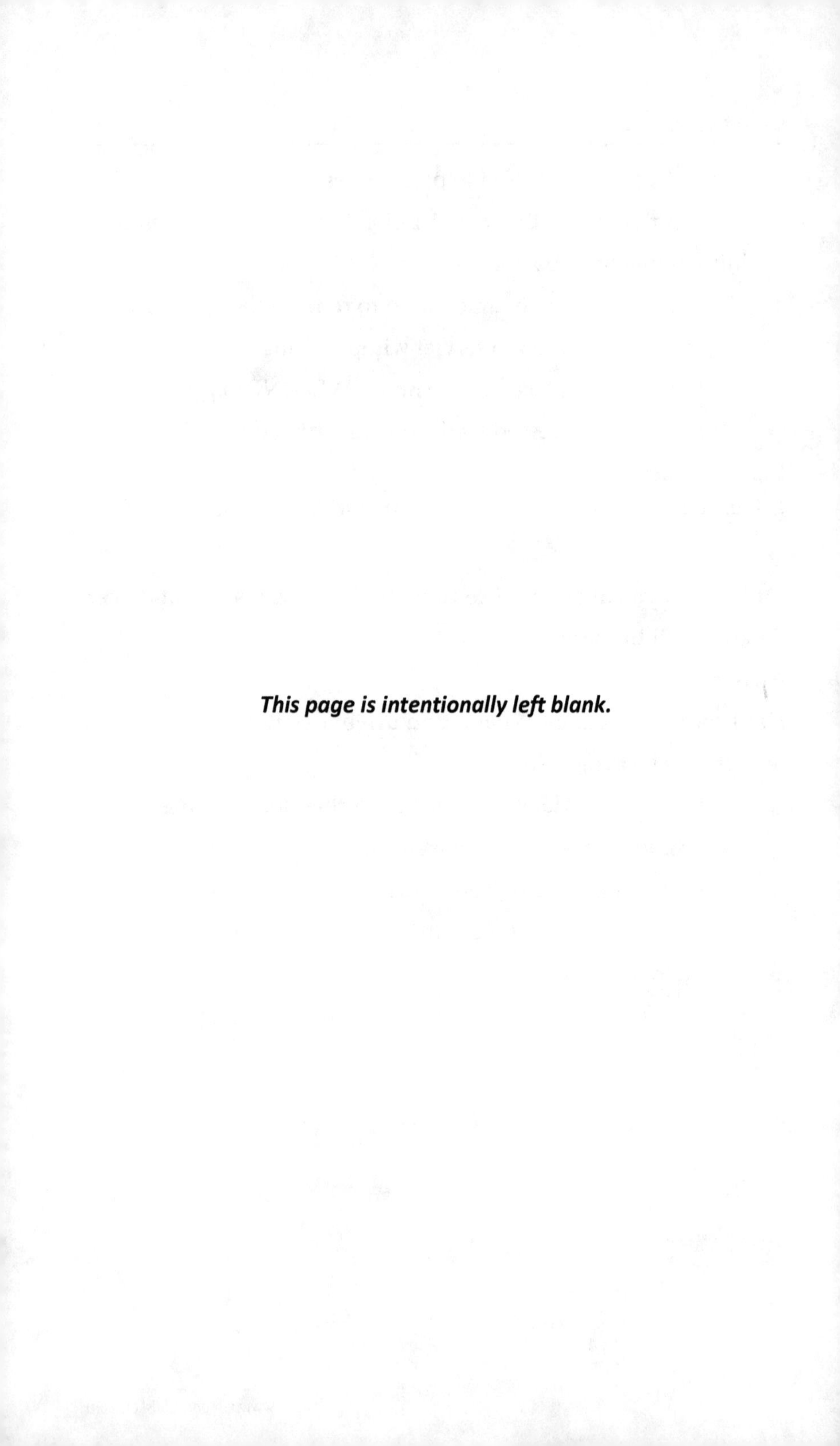

This page is intentionally left blank.

Chapter 5

Session Management

82: What is Session Timeout?

Answer:

Session Timeout is the time for which the web server waits before it invalidates a particular session which is inactive. By default, the tomcat server's session timeout is 30 minutes, meaning, if the session is inactive for 30 minutes, the server invalidates the session and any requests associated with the session. You can set the Session Timeout of your servlet in 2 ways – by setting the session-timeout tag to the number of minutes for which to wait for activity within the session-config tag or by using the setMaxInactiveInterval(<seconds>) method of HttpSession object. So to set the timeout to 10 minutes, it is either

<session-config> <session-timeout>10</session-timeout> </session-config>

in the web.xml Or

HttpSession.setMaxInactiveInterval(600)
The xml tag considers the value in minutes while the session object's method expects the value in seconds.

83: Explain the pros and cons of Session Management with Cookies.

Answer:

Cookies help store crucial user information and settings on the client-browser. The servler accesses the cookies to retrieve the information stored in them regarding the previous browsing and other preferences. But session management with cookies are not recommended because of the following reasons. Cookies are stored on the client's browser. So if the user decides to delete the existing cookies and not to allow any cookies further by disabling cookies in the browse, then your session management goes for a toss! Moreover, cookies only work for HTTP protocol. While this is the most common and popular protocol used in the Internet, it is definitely not the ultimate one.

84: Explain the different milestones of a session.

Answer:

A session passes through some important milestones while it exists. The lifecycle milestones of a session are when a session is created and when it is destroyed. The attribute milestones are when a new attribute is added, removed or replaced during the session. The migration milestones of a session are when the session is about to become passive when it migrates to another virtual machine and when the session is just activated, migrating from a different virtual machine. You can use the session event listeners to manipulate these session milestones.

85: Of the available four session management techniques available in JSP, which one is the most preferred and why?

Answer:

Sessions can be managed with cookies, hidden fields, HttpSession object, or URL Rewriting. Choosing a single best option from these may not cover all the possible situations. Ideally, a combination is chosen so that if one fails, the other takes over. Cookies are definitely the most widely used session management techniques. But since cookies can be disabled by the client browser, this technique is not fully dependable. So the programmers usually either use URL Rewriting or Session objects depending on the application's requirements. With URL Rewriting, the issues spotted are that they are not as secure and can become cumbersome when having to manage very long page addresses. Moreover, the URL has to be generated dynamically to append the session id which may not be possible from static HTML pages. The main advantage of URL Rewriting is that it takes over the control only if the browser's cookies are disabled. HttpSession objects are a comparatively safer option even though there's a lot of coding involved in the server side to effect the same.

86: Explain the scope of session timeout set in the web.xml file.

Answer:

In the web.xml, the session timeout is set in minutes. Its scope is for an application. For the entire web application, the session timeout set in the web.xml file will be considered. If the session timeout is set to 10 minutes in web.xml, for each session, the server checks the timeout interval from the time the particular session was last accessed and if it exceeds 10 minutes, the session is closed and all data related to the session are removed from the memory. So for all sessions in the application, the session timeout will be 10 minutes, unless otherwise specified in the program dynamically. Each browser has a different session and hence, opening the same URL from different browsers with the same login will be considered as different sessions. Similarly, each system has a different session and hence, even if you use the same browser from a different system, it will be treated as a different session.

87: What are the different ways for Session Tracking in JSP?

Answer:

The different ways for session tracking in JSP are:

a) **Cookies**: HTTP cookies are the small information about a session created by the server and stored on the client side
b) **URL Rewriting:** Session data will be stored/appended in the end of each URL
c) **Hidden form fields:** Session information can be stored in hidden form fields and it will be included in GET and POST data
d) **HttpSession:** Session data can be stored in session implicit object using session.setAttribute() and retrieved by session.getAttribute().Since it is stored in server, session object should not have huge amount of data

88: What is URL rewriting?

Answer:

When a client sends a request to the server, some extra information/parameters will be appended to the URL. This is URL rewriting. Session id will be included with the URL during session tracking. URL has a size limitation.

http://localhost:8080/Servlet1/loginServlet?sessionid=123456

89: What are cookies?

Answer:

Cookies are small pieces of information that are stored on the client side by a server. It is sent to the client along with the response and will be sent back to the server along with the next request to maintain the session. We can store only String information within the cookie. If the cookie is disabled in the browser, it will not work.

Client >> request1 >>Server >>response + cookie >> Client >> request2 + cookie >> Server

90: What will happen if the cookies at the client side are disabled and how can we handle the session?

Answer:

If cookies are disabled, it will append the session id/details to the URL otherwise it will take it from cookies. We can store only String information within the cookie. If the cookie is disabled in the browser, it will not work.

We can handle the session using encodeURL() method through which we can obtain URL Rewriting mechanism.

String url= "/agent/login";

String encodedURL= response.encodeURL(url); (OR)

<ahref="<%=
response.encodeRedirectURL("http://www.google.com")%<">Goo
gle.com </a>

91: What methods are available in a Cookie and what are they used for?

Answer:

The methods that are available in a Cookie and their uses are:

a) **Public void addCookie(Cookie cookie):** To add cookies in the HttpServletResponse object
b) **Public Cookie[] getCookies():** To retrieve all the cookies from the browser (HttpServletRequest object)
c) **Public void setMaxAge(intcookieExpiry):** To get maximum age of the cookie (lifetime)
d) **Public String getName():** To get name of the cookie. We cannot change the cookie name once it is created
e) **Public String getValue():** To retrieve the value stored in the cookie

92: What is session activation and session passivation?

Answer:

a) **Session activation:** Session which is persisted, would be retrieved to memory from the persistent storage
b) **Session passivation:** When a session is inactive, it would be written in persistent storage

93: What is Session Tracking and how would you track a user session in Servlets?

Answer:

Session Tracking is a mechanism used by the servlets to maintain multiple reques details from the same user within the session. The methods used for session tracking are:

a) Cookies
b) URL Rewriting
c) HttpSession
d) Hidden form fields

94: What is the difference between URL, URI and URN?

Answer:

The differences between URL, URI and URN are:

a) **URI(Uniform Resource Identifier):** It is a resource locator. It identifies the resource using its name or location, or both. But it will not define how the resource can be obtained. This type of URI can also be called URN
b) **URN(Uniform Resource Name):** Identifies a resource independent of its location.It would define a namespace but not define the location.
<xsd:schemaxmlns="http://www.w3.org/2001/XMLSchema" xmlns:xsd="http://www.w3.org/2001/XMLSchema" nspace="http:ex"
c) **URL(Uniform Resource Locator):** A subset of URI which is an identifier for some resources. URL provides information such as from where or how the resource is obtained

For example: http://www.google.com

95: How would you destroy a session in a servlet?

Answer:

We can destroy the current session in a servlet using invalidate() method. E.g. session.invalidate()

96: How would you invalidate a current session?

Answer:

A current session can be invalidated by setting the timeout value in web.xml as below:

Session will be invalidated in 20 minutes.

<session-config>

<session-timeout> 20 </session-timeout>

</session-config>

Session will be invalidated programmatically using session.setMaxInactiveInterval() method in servlets/jsp.

public void setMaxInactiveInterval(inttimeoutInterval)

97: Do we need to serialize the objects that will be stored in HttpSession?

Answer:

Yes. Httpsession is used to store the user information. By default Session objects will be maintained in the memory. All objects that need to be stored in httpsession should be serialized (implements java.io.Serializable interface) to avoid data loss.Servlet Container/application server would expect the session object to be serialized. Otherwise NotSerializableException may occur. The attributes/fields, which are not required to be persisted should be declared as transientto avoid serializing unnecessary objects. It will reduce the time to be taken for persisting the session objects and cost of serialization.

98: How would you refresh the session objects if the user has logged off from the account but had not closed the browser?

Answer:

Session will act on user's browser and does not depend on whether the user is logged on/off. If the user is logged off but the browser is not closed, the session object should be refreshed/removed. Otherwise, same session data (like user search input details) will be repeated for the next user. So we can remove the session object programmatically when the user gets logged off.

```
public class LogoutServlet extends HttpServlet {
public void doGet(HttpServletRequestreq,
HttpServletResponseresp)
throwsServletException, IOException {
    HttpSessionhttpSession = request.getSession(false);
if (httpSession!= null)
        {
httpSession.invalidate();
        }
        // log off code here...
    }
}
```

99: How would you configure session time out values in servlets and JSP?

Answer:

Users can configure session time value by manually setting the session time out value. But it should be a sensible value. If the session time out value is small, user information will be lost before their transaction is completed. If the session value is large, memory overhead will be increased since the session will contain many users' data for that time period. It is better to leave the default session time out value as 30 minutes (or 25). We can configure the time out value in JSP and servlets, but it would be applicable for the current session. We can also configure it in web.xml.

In web.xml:

```
<session-config>
<session-timeout>30</session-timeout>
</session-config>
```

In JSP:

```
<%session.setMaxInactiveInterval(30*60)%>
```

In Servlet:

```
HttpSession session = request.getSession(true);
session.setMaxInactiveInterval(30*60)
```

100: What is the difference between request.getSession(true) and request.getSession(false)?

Answer:

The difference between request.getSession(true) and request.getSession(false) are:

a) **getSession(true):** Will check if any session already exists for this user. If a session exists, it will return the session object; else it will create a new session and return it.

b) **getSession(false):** Will check if any session already exists for this user. If a session exists, it will return the session object, else it will return null. It is used when the user needs to logout i.e. request for session to be invalidated or timing out.

101: How would you set and delete a cookie from the Servlet?

Answer:

Create a cookie and add it in the response object. To delete it, set the cookie age as zero using setMaxAge() method and add it in the response object.

a) **To add a cookie:**
```
Cookie cookie = new Cookie("username", "abc");
response.addCookie(cookie);
```
b) **To delete a cookie:**
```
cookie.setValue("username", null);
cookie.setMaxAge(0);
response.addCookie(cookie);
```

102: Name the different ways of Session tracking in servlets.

Answer:

The different ways of session tracking in servlets are:

a) Cookies
b) HttpSession
c) URL Rewriting
d) Hidden Form Fields

103: What mechanisms are used by the servlet container to store the session information?

Answer:

The various mechanisms used by the servlet container to store the session information are:

a) Cookies
b) URL rewriting
c) Hidden form fields
d) SSL (using HTTPS protocol) Sessions

104: How would you handle session tracking in JSP pages if the user browser has disabled the cookies?

Answer:

If the browser has disabled cookies, session tracking in JSP pages can be handled as below:

a) Using URL Rewriting, the session id would be appended in the end of each link as a name-value pair
b) Using response.encodeURL() method, session id can be appended with a given URL
c) Using response.encodeRedirectURL() method in case of redirection
d) These methods will automatically check whether the cookies are supported by the browser. If browser supports them, the URL will remain unchanged since the session details will be available in cookies. If it is not, it will append the session id with the URL and the target/next JSP would be able to retrieve this session details
<%@page session="true" %>

```
<% session.setAttribute("name",name);
    String name = response.encodeURL("target.jsp");
%>
```

105: What is the maximum cookie size and how many cookies we can store in response object?

Answer:

Maximum Cookie size is 4kb and a maximum of 20 cookies can be stored in response object.

106: How would you set inactivity lease period on a per-session basis?

Answer:

After creating session, inactivity lease period can be set using setMaxInactiveInterval() method. Session will be inactive after some amount of time which is defined in seconds in this method.

```
<%
session.setMaxInactiveInterval(180);
%>
```

107: What are the ways to destroy a session?

Answer:

The different ways to destroy a session are:

a) If it times out
b) Using invalidate() method on session object
c) If the application stops responding (crashes) or application is un-deployed

108: Which session tracking mechanism does not have a size limit and which has good performance?

Answer:

The different tracking mechanisms and their size limits are:

a) **Session:** No limit on size of session data - Good in performance
b) **Hidden Fields:** No limit on size of session data
c) **Cookies:** There is limit for cookie size
d) **URL Rewriting:** There is a size limit for storing data
e) **Persistent storage:** No limit for keeping session data

109: What is the use of setSecure() and getSecure() methods in Cookies?

Answer:

The uses of setSecure() and getSecure() methods in Cookies are:

a) **setSecure():** Indicates to the client/web browser that the cookies must be sent over secure protocol (HTTPSor SSE) when it sends cookies to the server
    i) mycookie.setSecure(true): send cookies to server when secure protocol is being used
    ii) mycookie.setSecure(false): send cookies over any protocol
b) **getSecure():** Indicates whether the browser is sending cookies over secure protocol or not
    i) boolean b = getSecure()
    ii) return true: browser is sending cookies over secure protocol
    iii) return false: sending over any protocol

110: How would you prevent a JSP page from creating a session automatically?

Answer:

By changing the JSP page directive's session attribute to false, we can prevent a JSP page from creating a session automatically. By default this is set to true.

```
<%@ page session="false">
```

111: What is the use of setComment() and getComment() methods in Cookies?

Answer:

Comment is the optional attribute describing the Cookie's purpose. This is set using setComment() and retrieved using getComment().

a) mycookie.setComment("this is test comment");

b) System.out.println(mycookie.getComment());

This page is intentionally left blank.

Chapter 6

Session Object

112: What are the differences between cookies and sessions?

Answer:

Cookies are used for session management and hence, the terms are used interchangeably by some people. But actually cookies and sessions are totally different objects even though cookies help the session object in managing client sessions. The main difference between a cookie and a session is that a cookie stores the session details in the client browser while the session contains the same information in the servlet server. Essentially, both contain the same information regarding one session. The difference is where it is stored. Moreover, cookies have limited attributes and size whereas the session object does not have any limit on its size. If you delete a cookie, you are deleting information regarding your session and hence, the corresponding session information will also be deleted. While the cookies are stored in the browser for each user, the session functions for each login since that's when the server identifies the user and tries to fetch a cookie corresponding to the user. Once the user logs out, the session's data is lost unless it is made persistent. But as long as the cookies are not disabled or deleted, the information remains intact in the client browser.

113: Why should we create our own cookies instead of using the browser cookies?

Answer:

Cookies are a way to store the user information or the session information on the client browser. But the user can delete cookies or disable them citing a possible vulnerability to online hackers. To combat this situation, the session details are made persistent by writing the cookies into a file or database. This further provides a lot of other important possibilities for session management. Even though you can make your session persistent in memory, there's a risk involved when the web server fails. To avoid all sorts of risks, the cookies are made persistent by writing the session details into a file or database. It has to be noted that long-term and very short-term cookies are not to be entertained.

114: How can you make the session persistent?

Answer:

Sessions can be made persistent in different ways – in memory, in file and in database or as a browser cookie. When you are storing the session details on the web server's memory, it is in-memory persistence. The risk here is that, if the web server fails and is restarted, the session details are lost. When you are using cookies that are stored in the client browsers, there's a risk of deleting or disabling the cookies and you lose the session details. So the more persistent ways are to write in a file or in the database. When you are making the session persistent in file, you have to set the *persistent-store-type* parameter to *file* and specify the directory where the session files are stored under the *persistent-store-dir* in the weblogic.xml file. Make sure that you create the directory mentioned as *persistent-store-dir* and give required permissions to write the session details. For JDBC Persistence, set the *persistent-store-type* parameter to *jdbc* and *persistent-store-pool* to the database connection pool. Also you have to create and maintain the *wl_servlet_sessions* database in the database server.

115: What are the real-time circumstances when the session ends?

Answer:

In real-time, the session can end in many ways. The most common way in which a session is ended by the user explicitly is when the user logs out of the application. During logoff, the session is explicitly closed and all memory allocations with regard to the session are released. When the session remains inactive over a period of time, to be more precise, beyond the session timeout set in the web.xml, the session closes. Another instance is when the user closes the browser, the session is closed too. If the user closes the particular web application and the browser does not support cookies, the session is lost. One more instance is when the session is invalidated in the program.

116: How do you implement single sign-on for multiple applications?

Answer:

When there are multiple web applications that are related to the same user, a implementing a single sign-on will be the best option. If you want to implement the logic of a single logoff for all the web applications, there's no single direct option available in the servlet API. But using the following 3 functions one after the other will explicitly effect logging off the user from all web applications. The weblogic.servlet.security.ServletAuthentication class has 3 methods that help logging off the user in single sign-off. The logout() method in this class logs out the user from the web application. But only the user authentication details are removed and the session remains live. So the next method invalidateAll() is called which invalidates all currently open sessions and cookies for the current user. The last step is to call the killCookie() method that invalidates the cookie and it is deleted as soon as the request is sent to the server.

117: How will you store and retrieve your form data into session objects?

Answer:

To store data into a session object we can use setAttribute() method.

```
session.setAttribute("firstName",firstName);
```

To retrieve data from the session object we can use getAttribute() method of session object.

```
String fName = (String) session.getAttribute("firstName);
```

118: You would like to update your account profile details. Where should you enter your username and profile password again? How should we verify if this username is the same as the logged in username?

Answer:

The user name verification to update account details is carried out as follows:

a) **Login.jsp:** It contains the form to be filled.

b) **LoginProcess.jsp**

```
<%
    String userName =
    request.getParameter("userName");
    session.setAttribute("userName",userName);
%>
```

c) **Profile.jsp:** Enter username again in the profile page form.

d) **ProfileValidation.jsp**

```
<%
//profile page username
String uName = request.getParameter("uName");
String userName= (String)
session.getAttribute("userName);
if (uName.equals(username) {
    System.out.println("You are authorized");
}
%>
```

119: What is the default Session status in a JSP page and how can it be changed?

Answer:

By default, the session is enabled in a JSP page which is not necessary. To disable the session, we need to explicitly give the option in page directive.

```
<%@ page session="false" %>
```

120: Request object will not be used to pass data from JSP to servlet. Then how can we achieve it?

Answer:

It can be achieved by the following methods:

a) We can pass it using session object and hidden field
b) Set data in session attribute using
   session.setAttribute("name", name)
   and retrieve it in Servlet file using
   String name = (String) session.getAttribute("name");
c) Pass the data as hidden field in JSPand retrieve it in servlet using
   <input type="hidden" name="name" value="name"> and
   String name = (String) request.getParameter("name");

121: Is there any size limitation for the data which is stored in a session object?

Answer:

No. There is no size limitation for the session data as the session would be stored on the server side. SessionId has a size limitation of approximately 4000 bytes as the session id may be stored in cookies or encoded in the URL (i.e. URL rewriting). Cookie size and HTTPrequest should not exceed 4kb.

122: How would you know if the http session is removed (when time outs)?

Answer:

The class which needs to be stored in session objects should implement HttpSessionBindingListener interface (javax.servlet.http package) and override valueUnbound() and valueBound() methods to know if the http session is removed. If the session is timed out or removed, the servlet container will invoke the valueUnbound() method on the class object. If this class object is stored into the session for the next user valueBound() method will be invoked.HttpSessionBindingListener interface is used to track the session events on the particular object.

public void valueBound(HttpSessionBindingEventboundEvent)
public void valueUnbound(HttpSessionBindingEventunboundEvent)

123: How would you invalidate a session if the user closes the browser window?

Answer:

If the client browser is closed, the server would not be able to identify it. We can use client side validation to monitor browser window events and report to the servlet to invalidate it. Otherwise, the session will be invalidated automatically once it is timed out which is configured in the application. Therefore, if the next request comes from client to server, it will create a new session.

124: What will happen if an object gets unbound or bound to the

session?

Answer:

When an object gets bound or unbound to/from the session, the session will check whether the class implements HttpSessionBindingEvent interface. If it does implement, the servlet will notify the object about the event such as object is stored in the session/removed from the session. The session binds the object by invoking HttpSession.setAttribute() method and unbinds the object by invoking HttpSession.removeAttribute() method.

125: How many sessions would be created if a user sends requests to more than one component, or if a user opens 2 browser windows?

Answer:

Only one session will be created if the windows are in the same browser (e.g. IE), however, if different browsers are used (for instance IE and Firefox), then two sessions will be created.

126: What are the options available for deleting session data?

Answer:

The various options available for deleting session data are:

a) **Setting the session timeout:** Set the time out for the individual session using setMaxInactiveInterval() method. This time value is seconds
public void setMaxInactiveInterval(intmaxInterval)
b) **Deleting the entire session:** Delete the entire session using invalidate() method

public void invalidate()

c) **Configure web.xml:** Configure the session time out value in web.xml. This time value is minutes. If this value is retrieved in the servlet using getMaxInactiveInterval() method, it will return it in seconds

```
<session-config>
<session-timeout>5</session-timeout>
</session-config>
```

d) **Remove particular attribute:** Remove particular attribute or the value of a particular key using removeAttribute() on session object

public void removeAttribute(String param1)

e) **Log the user out:** Call logoutServlet to remove the client from the server and invalidate all the users' session

127: How would you delete all the sessions available on the server that are inactive for more than an hour?

Answer:

All the sessions that are inactive for more than an hour can be deleted as shown below:

```
public void doGet(HttpServletRequestreq,
HttpServletResponseresp)
throwsServletException, IOException {
PrintWriter out = resp.getWriter();
HttpSession session = req.getSession(true);
HttpSessionContext context = session.getSessionContext();
    Enumeration ids = context.getIds();
while (ids.hasMoreElements()) {
```

```
    String sid = (String)ids.nextElement();
HttpSession session = context.getSession(sid);
    Date isHourAgo = new Date(System.currentTimeMillis() -
    60*60*1000);
    Date dateAccessed = new
    Date(session.getLastAccessedTime());
if (dateAccessed.before(isHourAgo)) {
    session.invalidate();
    }
}
```

128: What is session hijacking?

Answer:

A hacker takes control of the session after obtaining or creating authentication session id/information. The hacker uses a brute forced session id to access the application session when session is still active. HTTP session attacking can be prevented using a secured HTTPS connection. This is session hijacking.

129: How would you know when the session is created and if it is last accessed or not?

Answer:

We can know when the session was created and if it was last accessed or not using:

a) **getCreationTime():** Shows creation time and session age. It is used to restrict the session to a fixed amount of time
b) **getLastAccessedTime():** Used to inform when the session was last accessed. i.e at what time the container received a

request in this session id

130: How would you know whether the session was already created or has just created?

Answer:

We would know whether the session was already created or had just been created using isNew() method of session. If session.isNew() returns true, it is new session. If it returns false, session was already created.

131: How would you access a preexisting session without creating a new session in a servlet?

Answer:

The request.getSession(false) method will return null if no session exists. If it does not return null, it is preexisting session.

132: What are the key milestones for a HttpSession object?

Answer:

The key milestones for a HTTPSession object are:

a) **Session lifecycle:** HttpSessionEvent and HttpSessionListener are used when the session is created and destroyed
b) **Session attribute lifecycle:** HttpSessionBindingEvent and HttpSessionAttributeListener are used when a session attribute is added, replaced, and removed
c) **Session migration:** HttpSessionEvent and HttpSessionActivationListener are used when the container is about to migrate the session from one JVM to

another JVM (session passivated) and when the container has just migrated the session into a different JVM (session activated)

133: What is the difference between setting session timeout programmatically and in the deployment descriptor?

Answer:

The difference between setting session timeout programmatically and in the deployment descriptor is:

a) **Deployment Descriptor:** Specified in minutes. Session will never expire if value is zero or less than zero
b) **Programmatically:** Specified in seconds. Session will never expire if value is a negative value

134: How will you retrieve all the session data in an application when you are not aware of any particular session data?

Answer:

All the session data in an application can be retrieved when we are not aware of any particular session data by the following methods:

a) Some data needs to be stored in session using session.setAttribute()
b) Using session.getAttributeNames() method, we can collect all the session attributes and store it in Enumeration which will return Enumeration of the session attributes
c) Using hasMoreElements() of Enumeration, we can iterate the session attributes
d) Using nextElement() of Enumeration, we can retrieve each

session attribute name

e) Using session.getAttribute(), we can retrieve the attribute value of the retrieved attribute names

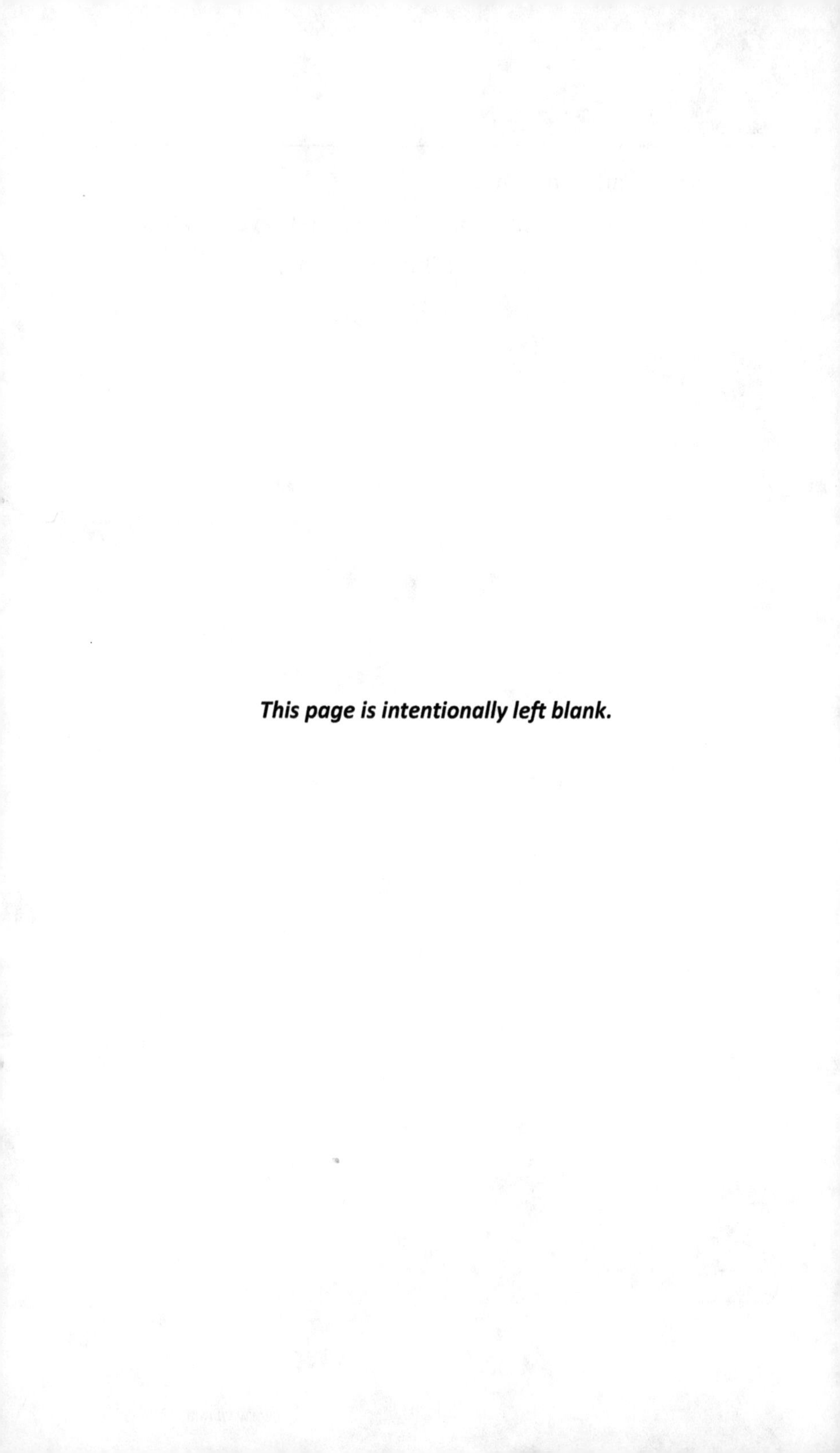

This page is intentionally left blank.

Chapter 7

Servlet Event Listeners

135: What is the use of Events Listeners in Servlets?

Answer:

Event listeners are used to monitor the changes being made to session, request, and servlet context objects. They are used to allow resource management and automated processing based on the event status.Tracking of events occurring in a web application is achieved through event listeners.

136: What are the events that can be monitored by Event Listeners?

Answer:

The following events can be monitored by Event Listeners:

a) Any changes to Servlet Context object such as adding, replacing, or removing attributes from ServletContext. i.e. changes in attributes and its lifecycle

b) Any changes to a Servlet Session object such as adding, replacing, or removing attributes
c) Creating a session, validating a session, or activating a session
d) Initializing a servlet and destroying the servlet by taking it out of service
e) Any changes to Request object such as requests coming in and going out of scope

137: What are the different types of events available in Servlets? (or) Which are the different levels in which events can be handled?

Answer:

The different levels in which events can be handled are:

a) **Request Level events:** Any changes to request objects
b) **Session level events:** Any changes to session objects
c) **ServletContext level events:** Any changes to Context parameters

138: What are the different types of Event Listeners available in Servlets?

Answer:

The different types of Event Listeners available in Servlets are:

a) **Request Listeners:** Notifies when a request comes into scope for the servlet or filters and goes out of scope for the servlet
b) **Session Listeners:** Notifies when an object is included into the session and when a session is created, destroyed,

timed out, or when an attribute is added or removed from the session

c) **Context Listeners:** Notifies when a context is created or destroyed from the application

139: Explain about Request level Event Listener interfaces.

Answer:

There are two types of interfaces available for handling request level events. They are:

a) **ServletRequestListener:** Notifies when a request comes into scope for the servlet and goes out of scope for the servlet

b) **ServletRequestAttributeListener:** Notifies when request attribute is changed (adding, replacing, removing)

140: What are the different types of interfaces available to handle ServletContextlevel events?

Answer:

There are two types of interfaces available for handling ServletContext level events. They are:

a) **ServletContextListener:** Notifies when the servlet is created and destroyed

b) **ServletContextAttributeListener:** Notifies when the servlet context attribute is changed (added, replaced or removed)

141: What are the different types of Event Listeners available for handling Session level events?

Answer:

The different types of Event Listeners available for handling Session level events are:

a) **HttpSessionListener:** Takes care of Session lifecycle changes. It notifies when the session is initialized or destroyed

b) **HttpSessionActivationListener:** Notifies when session objects move from one JVM to another. When the session object is migrating from one server to another, the sessionWillPassivate() method is called. This will be invoked when the session is about to be destroyed. Once the object has successfully migrated, the 'session has been activated' notification message will be received by the method sessionDidActivate().
It does not need to be configured in web.xml. When attributes are migrated, it must implement Serializable interface

c) **HttpSessionAttributeListener:** Notifies the changes in the HTTPsession attributes (adding, replacing, removing attributes).i.e. attributes which are added in the session

d) **HttpSessionBindingListener:** When an object is added or removed from the session, the container checks if the object class implements this interface and valueBound() and valueUnbound() method will be invoked accordingly. It does not need to be configured in web.xml

142: How would you access the session if you use event handling listener interfaces?

Answer:

Session can be accessed through event handling listener object using sessionCreated(HttpSessionEventsessionEvent) method as sessionEvent.getSession().

143: A class implements HttpSessionBindingListener and its object is stored in session. If the session is invalidated what will happen?

Answer:

If the session is invalidated, it will call valueUnbound() method where we would write the code to handle what needs to be done after the session is invalidated.

This page is intentionally left blank.

Chapter 8

Servlet Filter

144: What is a ServletFilter and what is it used for?

Answer:

A ServletFilter is an object that modifies the request header/request data and response header/response data. It intercepts the request before it goes to the servlet. For instance, after login.jsp, it goes to the servletfilter, which provides authorization. It also intercepts and modifies the response after it comes from the servlet.

145: What is the difference between a Servlet and a Filter?

Answer:

The difference between a Servlet and a Filter is that:

a) A Servlet acts like a controller which controls the request and response

b) A Filter is not a Servlet. It modifies the request and

response object based on some conditions. We can use it for auditing, authentication, logging, or when any modification needs to be made to request and response objects

146: What are Filter lifecycle methods?

Answer:

The Filter lifecycle methods are:

a) void init(FilterConfigfconfig) throws ServletException
b) void doFilter(ServletRequestreq, ServletResponse res, FilterChain chain) throws IOException, ServletException
c) void destroy()

147: Explain the ServletFilter lifecyle.

Answer:

The ServletFilter lifecycle is explained as follows:

a) The server calls init() method to initialize configuration object of the filter before it goes into service. FilterConfig interface contains methods to retrieve initialization parameters, filter's name, and the servlet context.
b) doFilter() method is called and filter receives request, response, and filterChain.

```
public void doFilter(ServletRequest request,
        ServletResponse response,
        FilterChain chain)
```

c) destroy() method is called when the filter has to be taken out of service.

It is similar to servlet lifecycle.

148: How to transfer control from one filter to another?

Answer:

All the filters which are given in the Filterchain will be executed by chain.doFilter(req, resp) method. If the calling filter is the last filter in the chain, the container will call the next resource/doXxx() method to process further and return to the last chain, transferring the control.

Filter1 >> Filter2 >> Servlet1(After execution) >> Filter2 >> Filter1 >> Container return the response to the client.

149: What are the interfaces available in ServletFilter?

Answer:

The various interfaces available in ServletFilter are:

a) javax.servlet.Filter
b) javax.servlet.FilterChain
c) javax.servlet.FilterConfig

150: What is FilterChain?

Answer:

FilterChain is the interface in which a series of filters are executed sequentially. It has to be configured in the deployment descriptor web.xml.

Subsequent filters are called using chain.doFilter(req, resp) method.

<filter>

<filter-name>filter1</filter-name>

```
<filter-class>com.servlet.filter1</filter-class>
</filter>
<filter>
<filter-name>filter2</filter-name>
<filter-class>com.servlet.filter2</filter-class>
</filter>
<filter-mapping>
<filter-name>filter1</filter-name>
<url-pattern>/servlet1</url-pattern>
</filter-mapping>
<filter-mapping>
<filter-name>filter2</filter-name>
<url-pattern>/servlet1</url-pattern>
</filter-mapping>
<servlet>
<servlet-name>servlet1</servlet-name>
<servlet-class>com.servlet.Servlet1</servlet-class>
</servlet>
<servlet-mapping>
<servlet-name>servlet1</servlet-name>
<url-pattern>/servlet1</url-pattern>
</servlet-mapping>
```

151: How would you access the ServletContext parameter in your filter init() method?

Answer:

The ServletContext parameter in filter init() method could be accessed as follows:

```
privateServletContextservletContext;
public void init(FilterConfigfilterConfig) {
    servletContext = filterConfig.getServletContext();
}
```

152: How would the servlet container invoke the filters?

Answer:

Filter is an object that modifies request and response objects. Filter should be configured in web.xml. It is mapped with the Servlets so as to be called before the servlet and after it has sent a response.

This page is intentionally left blank.

Chapter 9

JSP and Servlet

153: What is the difference between JSP and a servlet?

Answer:

The differences between JSP and a servlet are:

a) JSP is dynamic where we can incorporate Java code
b) Servlet is static where we can incorporate HTML code. i.e. HTML code in Java file. It is pure Java class
c) Servlet is faster than JSP because the first JSP page should be translated into a Java class file. It will maintain security
d) JSP can only support HTTP protocol whereas servlets can support various protocols

154: Why would you require calling a JSP page from servlet?

Answer:

We would require calling a JSP page from a servlet:

a) To navigate to presentation layer
b) If we want to send/output of any binary data such as images and PDFs from JSP, then JspWriter is not the most suitable method as it preserves unnecessary white-spaces in the binary data, meaning the browser will receive unwanted new line characters in the middle or end of the binary data. Additionally, a method to write binary data is not available in JspWriter
c) <% out.getOutputStream().write(...some binary data...) %>

155: How would you make a JSP generated servlet subclass the custom servlet class instead of using the default one?

Answer:

a) All JSP generated servlet classes implement HttpJspPage interface (if http protocol) or Jsp Page interface.
b) HttpJspPage contains service() method which will in turn call _jspService() method.
c) Since HttpJspPage contains _jspService() method, we cannot override the same method explicitly in the JSP. It will cause a compile time error as there are two methods with the same name and signature
d) All methods in the custom servlet should be final and it should contain service() method which would call _jspService() method, init() method has to invoke jspInit() method, and destroy() method has to invoke jspDestroy() method. However, it is not advisable to override these methods because the advanced optimization provided by the JSP engine may be lost

e) If these methods are not overridden, the JSP engine will give a translation error. If custom servlet is developed, JSP can extend it as below.

%@page extends="com.java.CustomServlet" %

156: If JSP page "login.jsp" contains an instance variable as "String name" and the "chgPwd.jsp" file also contains an instance variable as "String name". What will happen if the client requests login.jsp?

Answer:

If the client requests login.jsp, a compilation error will be given because the same variables are declared/used twice. When a JSP page (chgPwd.jsp) is included statically, the included page content will also become part of the main JSP page (login.jsp). Therefore, it will give a compilation error if both files use the same variables.

157: What is the use of inter-servlet communication?

Answer:

The uses of inter-servlet communication are:

a) **Servlet Collaboration:** Sharing of specific information between servlets
b) **Servlet reuse:** Reusing one servlet's public methods in another servlet
c) **Direct servlet manipulation:** Access other currently loaded servlets to perform specific tasks using servletcontext.

E.g. getServletContext().getServlet("writeServlet");

158: How do we use JDB logger in a JSP page?

Answer:

We use JDB logger in a JSP page as below:

```
<%@page import="java.util.logging.Logger" %>
<% Logger jsplogger =
Logger.getLogger(this.getClass().getName());%>
<c:forEach var="i" begin="1" end="10" step="1" >
<%
jsplogger.info();
%>
</c:forEach>
```

159: Describe the difference between 2-tier and 3-tier architecture.

Answer:

a) **2-tier architecture:** Client-Server model
Client will send request to the server, which will fetch the data from the client and send response back to client. Testing includes client user interface for the front-end and backend database. However, the server cannot send a response to multiple client requests

b) **3-tier architecture:** Multi-tier architecture
Client will send a request to the server, which will forward this request to the database. The database will send the data to server based on the request; the server will then forward this data to client. Testing includes UI, functionality, and database testing

Chapter 10

JSP Lifecycle and Methods

160: Describe the various stages of JSP life cycle.

Answer:

The various stages of JSP life cycle are:

a) **Translation:** When a browser makes a request for a JSP page for the first time, the JSP page is translated into a Java Servlet file. It will check for JSP syntax errors, add all included JSP files, and omits JSP and HTML comments. For example "Login.jsp" file would be translated to "Login_jsp.java", which is a servlet file

b) **Compilation:** This Java file is compiled using the javac compiler like normal Java files, and the class file is generated. If <load-on-startup> tag is configured in web.xml, the container would not wait for the first request to be made. It will start the compilation when the server/application gets started

c) **Initialization:** jspInit() method will be called only once by the container for a servlet instance. Every JSP page will have a separate servlet file. It will take care of getting resources and initializing variables declared in the JSP page
d) **Execution:** jspService() method will be called by the container for each request. It will take Request and Response objects as parameters. We cannot override this method. All scriptlets and expressions will be put into this method during the Translation phase
e) **Destruction:** jspDestroy() method is the last method called by the container. This will release all the resources acquired in jspInit() method. This method is similar to java finalize() method and cannot be certain when it will run and when the resource will be released

161: What are the JSP lifecycle methods and can we override these methods?

Answer:

The JSP lifecycle methods are:

a) jspInit()
b) _jspService()
c) jspDestroy()

We can override jspInit() and jspDestroy() methods but cannot override _jspService() method.

162: Why can't we override _jspService() method?

Answer:

We cannot override _jspService() method because:

The contents of our JSP page will go to _jspService() method, which means that this method is implicitly implemented

a) If we explicitly override this method, the compiler will give the error "the method is already implemented and cannot override"

163: How do we override jspInit method and where can we do it?

Answer:

jspInit method is overridden as follows:

```
<%!
    public void jspInit(){
        ServletConfigconfig= getServletConfig();
    }
%>
```

It can be overridden in the JSP Declaration tag.

164: How do we override jspInit() lifecycle method in the JSP page and pass initialization parameters to JSP?

Answer:

We can override jspInit() lifecycle method in JSP page using the JSP declaration tag <%! ... %>. Config object can be retrieved from getServletConfig() method and initialization parameters can be retrieved using getInitParameter() method of ServletConfig.

165: Can JSP be considered as an extensible technology?

Answer:

Yes. It can be extended using the development of custom tags which are available / encapsulated in tag libraries.

166: Describe the JSP translation phase.

Answer:

All included JSP that use included directives will be converted to single servlet. Variable declaration or <jsp:usebean> for the same bean cannot be used in both main JSP and included JSP since it is considered as a single unit. This is JSP translation phase.

167: How would you stop the execution of JSP in the middle of processing a request?

Answer:

We can stop the execution of JSP in the middle of processing a request using return statement. Once the JSP is compiled to a servlet all the statements will go inside the service() method so execution can be stopped using the return statement at any time.

168: How would you create static data in the jspInit() method?

Answer:

Static data can be created in jspInit() method as it only gets created once in the JSP's lifetime and is used in _jspService() method that is being called for every request, to pass the data to the client request.

When sending large amounts of data, this method will improve performance. However, we would create static and dynamic data from the JSP page that will be included in _jspService() method, this will be called for every request. There is no need to create static data every time for every request of the JSP page.

```
<%!
    char[] staticHeader1;
    StringBuffer sb1 = null;
    public void jspInit(){
        sb1 = new StringBuffer();
        sb1.append("<html>");
        sb1.append("<head><title>Static Data </title></head>");
        sb1.append("<body>");
        staticHeader1 = sb1.toString().toCharArray();
    }
%>
out.print(staticHeader1);
```

169: Why does JSP lifecycle method _jspService() start with an underscore ('_') while other methods do not?

Answer:

All the contents of the JSP page will be placed in _jspService() method by the JSP engine/container, we can't override this method. Hence it contains an underscore ('_') while other methods which can be overridden and do not have an underscore.

170: How can we use jspDestroy() method in an optimized way?

Answer:

jspDestroy() is only called once in the JSP lifecycle when the container/JSP engine removes the servlet from memory. To avoid memory leaks, we should close/remove all resources such as database connections, files, sockets, and instance variables within this method.

This page is intentionally left blank.

Chapter 11

JSP Implicit Object

171: What are the JSP implicit objects used for?

Answer:

The JSP implicit objects are used for handling server side objects such as request, response, and session objects.

a) **request:** javax.servlet.http.HttpServletRequest interface
   Handles request sent by client
   To retrieve query string, request parameters, request attributes, and header information
b) **response**: javax.servlet.http.HttpServletResponse interface
   Handles response that is sent to client
   To add cookie information, set the response content type, and redirect the response
c) **session**: javax.servlet.http.HttpSession interface
   To store the session information for a user/client
d) **out**: javax.servlet.jsp.JspWriter class

To send the output/content to the client

e) **application**: javax.servlet.ServletContext interface
To set and get application specific information

f) **Exception**: java.lang.Throwable class
To handle the error page in which an exception occurred

g) **config**: javax.servlet.ServletConfig
To retrieve servlet initialization parameters given in web.xml

h) **page**: java.lang.Object class
To access any of the servlet methods. However this page object should be type casted to servlet type.
It represents the current JSP page and sends the reference ("this") to the servlet which implements this JSP page.
It is not advisable to use page object as it consumes a large amount of memory.

i) **pagecontext**: javax.servlet.jsp.PageContext abstract class
To share information among different resources
It contains context specific information in different scopes and provides methods to set and get attributes.

172: Can we use implicit objects in a JSP Declaration tag?

Answer:

No. We cannot use implicit objects in a JSP Declaration tag as this would give a compilation error. Implicit objects are created by the web container and would be available within the _jspService method. It would not be available within any declarations.

```
<%!
public void method1(){
```

```
out.print("No Implicit Objects"); // Compilation error
}
%>
```

173: How would you pass implicit objects to the methods defined in the declaration tag?

Answer:

Implicit objects can be passed as Method Parameters to the methods defined in the declaration tag to make use of it.

```
<%!
    public String method1(HttpSession session) {
String s1 = (String)session.getAttribute("name");
    return s1;
}
%>
```

174: Why are all the JSP files present within WEB-INF except index.jsp?

Answer:

In order to protect web resources like JSP files, CSS, images, javascript files, and PDF files from direct access, we hide them in the WEB-INF directory which provides security. It is not accessible directly through the URL. So the request should go to the servlet for authenticating and authorizing the user before coming to JSP page or its resources.

175: How do you differentiate between a "pageContext" and "page" in JSP?

Answer:

The PageContext and Page in JSP differs in the following ways:

a) Page is the instance of the servlet corresponding to the JSP page. This JSP page is translated to the servlet class and the container makes an instance of the servlet to process the request of that page.
   It is the instance of jsp.HttpServletPage class of type java.lang.Object. So typecast is required when it is actually being used.
   ```
   <%=page.getServletInfo()%>// Error
   <%= ((servlet)page).getServletInfo() %>// Correct – typecasted
   <%= this.getServletInfo() %>// Correct – this refers to the current Object of the page
   ```
b) PageContext provides page related information such as characteristics of the page, access to the session, request and response objects, and access to the Out object's JspWriter. PageContext contains functions that can include another URL's contents and also methods to forward or redirect to a different URL when required. You can share data among different pages from a single translation unit.
   ```
   <% pageContext.forward("login.jsp") %>
   <% application = pageContext.getServletContext();%>
   <% config = pageContext.getServletConfig();%>
   <% session = pageContext.getSession();%>
   <% out = pageContext.getOut();%>
   ```

176: What is the default size of an "out" implicit object and what would you do if a large amount of data needs to be sent?

Answer:

The default size of an "out" object is 8kb, which is set in the "buffer" attribute of page directive. This can be increased if the data that needed to be sent exceeds 8kb.

<%@ page buffer="none|8kb|sizeinkb" %>

If the implicit object "out" is used in JSP, the container will include the JspWriter into the service() method. JspWriter is the buffered version of stream object and it is used to send character data to the client whereas ServletOutputStream is used to send binary data to the client.

This page is intentionally left blank.

Chapter 12

JSP Tags

177: What are the different tags available in JSP?

Answer:

The different tags available in JSP are:

a) **Directive tags:** Page, Include, and Taglib
b) **Action tags:** Forward, Include, and UseBean.
c) **Scriptlet tags:** Declaration, Scriptlet, and Expression

178: Can we declare methods within a JSP Declaration tag?

Answer:

Yes, we can declare methods within a JSP Declaration tag, but it is not a good practice. We can invoke the methods declared in a declaration tag from a Scriplet as well. However, JSP implicit objects cannot be used directly within declaration tags. It will give you a compilation error.

179: What is the use of <jsp:fallback> tag?

Answer:

This tag is specifically used when you need to create a HTML markup which has to be delivered if a plugin fails to start. The tag works such that, whenever a plugin fails to start, whatever message is given within the <jsp:fallback> tag is sent to the browser.

```
<jsp:plugin type="applet" code="applet1.class" codebase="/">
<jsp:params>
    <jsp:param name="param1" value="12345"/>
</jsp:params>
<jsp:fallback><b>Unable to load applet</b></jsp:fallback>
</jsp:plugin>
```

180: What is the nature of the variables declared in the Scriptlet tags and Declaration tags?

Answer:

Variables declared inside Scriptlet tags are declared directly into the _jspService method. Its scope is within the service method. This is the method that is called each time the JSP is accessed by the server. A JSP scriptlet's variable declaration is never threadsafe since they end up being instance variables in the servlet generated when the scriptlet runs. Instead of being within the _jspService() method called for every request, these variables end up being outside the method. Variable declared inside Declaration tags is considered as a global variable and is declared as an instance variable of the servlet class which was translated from the JSP. It is only made the first time JSP is accessed. Variable declared in the declaration tag is considered thread-safe since the variable is put in the generated servlet's _jspService() method as local variable.

181: How would you declare variables within the Scriptlet and Declaration tags? Explain with an example.

Answer:

a) **Declaration:**

```
<%!
java.util.Date date1 = new java.util.Date();
%>
current time :<%= date1 %>
```

Correct. Time will be different for each request.

b) **Scriptlet:**

```
<%
java.util.Datedate2 = new java.util.Date();
%>
current time :<%=date2%>
```

Wrong. Time will always be same for all requests.

182: What is the difference between JSP and HTML comments?

Answer:

The difference between JSP and HTML comments is:

a) **JSP Comment:** The JSP Engine will remove it during the translation phase. It will not be visible in the browser's View Source option, as it is not sent to the client. It is a hidden comment, only used by the developer

```
<%-- jsp comment --%>
```

b) **HTML Comment:** It is treated as all other HTML tags. It would be visible in browser's View source menu
<!-- html comment -->

183: How would you invoke a servlet from JSP or from another JSP?

Answer:

It can be invoked by using <jsp:include> tag or <jsp:forward> tag. If there are parameters to be passed we can use <jsp:param> tag within <jsp:forward> tag.

a) <jsp:include page="/com/myServlet/LoginServlet" flush="true" />
b) <jsp:forward page="/anotherPage.jsp" />

184: What are custom tags?

Answer:

Custom tags are:

a) User defined tags similar to JSP tags
b) Extensions to the JSP tags where the user can include their own tag library
c) Distributed in the custom tag library (jar file)
d) They are in the form of JSTL (Java standard tag library)
e) <%@ tagliburi="http://java.sun.com/jstl/core_rt" prefix="c" %>
<c:out> ... </c:out>

185: How does the JSP engine instantiate tag handler class instances?

Answer:

It will create/instantiate new tag handler instances every time a tag is encountered in a JSP page. Hence a pool of tag instances are maintained and reused. Whenever a tag is found, the JSP engine will find a new tag instance which is not being used, reuse it, and then release it.

This page is intentionally left blank.

Chapter 13

JSP Actions

186: What is the difference between JSP include action and include directive? What are they used for?

Answer:

The difference between JSP include action and include directive along with their uses are as follows:

a) **Include Directive:** <%@ include %>

<%@ include file="includeFile.jsp" %>

It is a Static include. All the included JSPfiles are compiled into a single servlet during translation and compilation stage. There is no Runtime performance overhead. You can use the Include directive to include both static and dynamic resources.

b) **Include Action**: <jsp:include>

<jsp:include page="includeFile.jsp" flush="true" />

It is a Dynamic include. All the JSPfiles are compiled into separate servlet files. These generated servlets would process

the request, and the content generated by them are included in the JSP response. It has run time performance overhead.
If you change the content of the jsp file used as an include file, it is automatically reflected the next time that include file is accessed. It is used only for dynamic resources.

187: What are the different actions available in JSP?

Answer:

The different actions available in JSP are:
jsp:include: To include other files
jsp:forward: To forward the control to another JSP/servlet
jsp:param: To pass parameters when including/forwarding
jsp:useBean: To use Java Bean class in the JSP
jsp:getProperty: To retrieve the bean fields/attributes in JSP
jsp:setProperty: To set the value to bean attributes from JSP
jsp:plugin: To include another plugin in JSPpage

188: When would JSP Actions and JSP Directives be processed?

Answer:

a) JSP Actions would be processed during the request processing stage. i.e. dynamically, at run time.
b) JSP Directives would be processed during the translation phase.

189: What are the scopes available for <jsp:usebean>?

Answer:

The scopes available for <jsp:usebean> are:

a) **Page:** Available only for the JSP page

b) **Request**: Available for JSP page and servlet (for forwarded jsp/servlet within request)
c) **Session**: Available for all JSP pages and servlet within that session
d) **Application**: Available for all JSP pages and servlet within the same application

190: How would you provide/pass data from the main JSP to an included JSP?

Answer:

Pass data can be provided from the main JSP to an included JSP by the code below:

```
<jsp:includepage="login.jsp">
    <jsp:param name="firstName" value="firstName" />
    <jsp:param name="lastName" value="lastName" />
</jsp:include>
```

191: Can we set value of page attribute in <jsp:include>?

Answer:

Yes, we can set value of page attribute in <jsp:include>:

a) Using request.getParameter().

```
<jsp:include
page="<%=request.getParameter("targetPage")%>"
    flush="true"/>
```

b) Using EL

```
<jsp:include page="${param.targetPage}" flush="true"/>
```

192: How would you pass values while forwarding control from one JSP to another JSP/servlet?

Answer:

Values can be passed while forwarding control from one JSP to another as follows:

```
<jsp:forward page="login.jsp">
    <jsp:param name="firstName" value="firstName" />
    <jsp:param name="lastName" value="lastName" />
</jsp:forward>
```

193: How would you generate an XML file from a JSP page?

Answer:

An XML file can be generated from a JSP file by the following steps:

a) Use contentType="text/xml" attribute of page directive
b) Write a bean class from where output should be populated into XML
c) createXml.jsp:

```
<%@ pagecontentType="text/xml;charset=ISO-8859-1" %>
<jsp:useBean id="createXml" class="createXmlFile"/>
<Person>
    <Person_Name><% out.print(createXml.getName());
    %></Person_Name>
    <Person_Age><% out.print(createXml.getAge());
    %></Person_Age>
</Person>
```

194: How would you use JavaBeans in JSP page?

Answer:

JavaBeans can be used in JSP page as shown below: <jsp:useBean

id="user" class="com.java.user" scope = "page | request | session | application "/>

a) <jsp:setProperty name = "user" property = "uname" value = "abc" / >

Name: which is mentioned in useBean id attribute

Property: property/field to be passed to the bean

Value: value of the property

b) <jsp:getProperty name = "user" property = "uname" />

c) To retrieve the bean value:

User Name: <%= user.getUname() %>

195: What will happen if you don't select the correct scope in the<jsp:useBean> tag?

Answer:

<jsp:useBean id="user" scope="page | request | session | application" />
The different types of useBean scope are page, request, session, and application. The default scope is "page".

Incorrectly specifying the scope will affect performance and increased memory overhead. The 'Request' scope would be more efficient than the 'Page' scope for multiple pages as 'Page' does not carry data over to the next page. If the 'Session' scope is used in place of the 'Request' scope, this will result in unnecessary memory usage, as the session object will stay in memory until explicitly removed or removed by the server after the configured time limit.

196: How would you pass information from one/main JSP to included JSP?

Answer:

Information can be passed from one JSP to included JSP as shown below:

```
<jsp:includepage="chgPwd.jsp" />
    <jsp:param name="uname" value="abc" />
    <jsp:param name="pwd" value="def" />
</jsp:include>
```

Chapter 14

GetParameter()

197: How will you retrieve the JSP form data into your JSP file?

Answer:

We can retrieve it by using getParameter() method of implicit request object.

```
<%
    String fname = request.getParameter("firstname");
    String lname = request.getParameter("lastname");
%>
```

198: What are the differences between request.getParameter() and request.getAttribute()?

Answer:

The differences between request.getParameter() and request.getAttribute() are:

a) **request.getAttribute():** Request attributes are the objects which are explicitly set in request object using request.setAttribute("name", name). If we have not set the values in request object using setAttribute(), values will not be available in request.getAttribute() method

b) **request.getParameter():** These are parameters received from JSP forms once the form/request is submitted. It can be strings which cannot be set but can be retrieved

199: Describe WAR/JAR/RAR/EAR files.

Answer:

a) **WAR (Web archive file):** Contains web components such as jsp, servlet, css, html, gif, and JPG
b) **JAR (Java Archive file):** Contains .classJava files. Used to implement libraries and plug-ins. A .Jar file cannot be placed inside another .Jar file
c) **EAR (Enterprise Archive):** Jar file with the extensions .ear. All relevant Jars that belong to the application can be placed inside the .ear file
d) **RAR (Resource Adapter Archive):** Can be placed inside an .ear file or can exist as a separate file

200: How do you retrieve Html form data from a JSP page?

Answer:

HTML form data can be retrieved from a JSP page using the following methods:

a) All the form fields can be accessed in JSP using getParameter() method on request object as String datatype
b) String s = request.getParameter("name"); // Within scriptlet tag

Chapter 15

Response Object

201: How would you send binary data in http response object?

Answer:

The getOutputStream() method of HttpServletResponse would be used to get an output streamobject that can be used to send the binary data in a HTTP response object.

202: How would you send the text output in the response object?

Answer:

The getWriter() method of HttpServletResponse would be used to get aPrintWriter object to send the text output in a response object.

203: How do you return a Http error in the response object?

Answer:

There are nine types of error codes available and it uses the sendError() method on request object.

response.sendError(HttpServletResponse.SC_NOT_FOUND); //Requested resource not available

response.sendError(HttpServletResponse.SC_SERVICE_UNAVAILABLE); //server temporarily unavailable.

204: What would you set the http error code to, in the response object within servlet?

Answer:

The HTTP error code is set to code 301 as it indicates permanent redirection. The new location will be set in the Location attribute of response header.

```
String url = response.encodeRedirectURL("...");
response.setStatus(HttpServletResponse.SC_MOVED_PERMANENTLY);
response.setHeader("Location", url);
```

205: How would you send a response from a Servlet to the client?

Answer:

Sending small amounts of data to the client can be done directly from the Servlet. However large amounts of data should be stored in a response object and sent to the JSP page, which will then display the output to the client.

a) **Send response through JSP:** using RequestDispatcher (Discussed already)
b) **Send response through servlet:** using PrintWriter

Sending response through servlet:

a) Set MIME type of the output using response.setContentType("text/html")

b) To send text output: Create PrintWriter object and call println() method

```
PrintWriter pw = response.getWriter();
pw.println("test");
```

c) To send binary output: Create ServletOutputStream object and call print() method

```
ServletOutputStreamsos =
response.getOutputStream();
sos.print(outb);
```

206: Why do we need to set Content length in the response object?

Answer:

The header content length needs to be set in the response object to avoid unnecessary network traffic and improve performance.

```
intleng;
response.setContentLength(leng);
```

When the client requests data from the server, it will establish a socket connection to receive the response from the server. If this includes large amounts of data, such as images, it has to create multiple connections. The number of connections depends on content length of the header and size of the content being received from the server. Therefore, the number of connections can be reduced based on the content length setting in the response object.

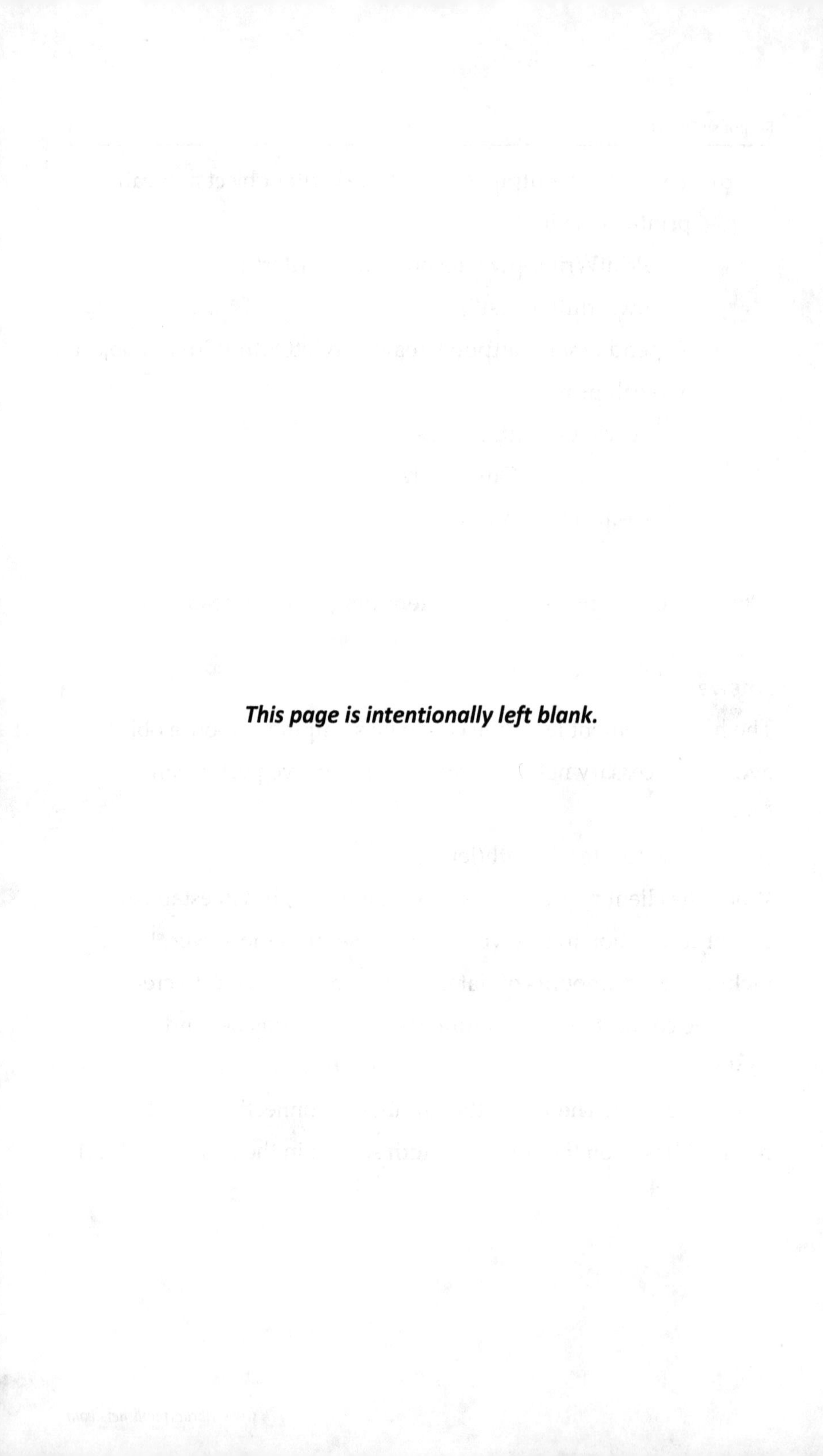

This page is intentionally left blank.

Chapter 16

PrintWriter, JspWriter

207: Compare JspWriter and PrintWriter.

Answer:

a) **JspWriter:** It is the buffered version of PrintWriter and denoted by "out" implicit object for sending output back to the client. It throws java.io.IOException. For example, if HTTP connection is broken for some reason, JSP would not send any data to the broken connection

b) **PrintWriter:** It does not support buffering and does not throw any exception. It is obtained from response.getWriter()

208: How can we write the JSP output to an Excel spreadsheet?

Answer:

JSP output can be written to an Excel spreadsheet by defining the contentType attribute of page directive to "application/vnd.ms-excel" in a JSP page. It will direct the output to the Excel sheet.

209: What will happen if you store request parameters in servlet context and pass it in PrintWriter object?

Answer:

The following might happen if you store request parameters in servlet context and pass it in PrintWriter object:

a) It will sometimes create different/wrong output as the servlet context will be accessible to all the servlets in an application. It can be updated by any servlet and may therefore generate the wrong output
b) Create PrintWriter object using response.getWriter() method
c) Get parameters using request.getParameters() and store it in context object using getServletContext().setAttribute()
d) Pass this context value in out.print() method using getServletContext().getAttribute() method

Chapter 17

Miscellaneous

210: How would you implement MVC (Model View Controller) design pattern in JSP-Servlet application?

Answer:

MVC (Model View Controller) design pattern is implemented in JSP-Servlet application by:

a) Creating a JSP form page
b) Creating a Servlet - **Controller**
c) Creating the Model (POJO class) - **Model**
d) Creating a deployment descriptor (web.xml)
e) Creating a JSP View - **View**

211: What are all the different types of exception handling mechanisms available in a JSP page?

Answer:

The different types of exception handling mechanisms available in a JSP page are:

a) **Exception implicit object:** run time exception handling
b) **Declarative exception:** Global exception handling

212: How would you handle run-time exceptions in JSP?

Answer:

To handle runtime exceptions in JSP, the relative URL should be given in "errorPage" attribute value.

This object would be available only to pages that have isErrorPage=true with the page directive.

```
<%@ page isErrorPage='true' %>
```

Test.jsp:

```
<%@page errorPage="ErrorPage.jsp" %>
<%
inti=5;
out.print(i/0);
%>
```

ErrorPage.jsp:

```
<%@ page isErrorPage='true' %>
<%
out.print("<h1> Divide by zero error</h1>");
out.print(exception.getMessage());
%>
```

213: How would you handle Declarative exception or how will you specify global error page in web.xml - deployment descriptor file?

Answer:

Declarative exceptions can be handled by the following methods:

a) We can configure exception-type or error code in the web.xml which will route the control to the JSP file that is given in the <location> tag.

```
<error-page>
    <exception-type>Exception</exception-type>
    <location> /errorExcp.jsp </location>
</error-page>
```

b) Error code 404 which is a browser HTTP error for "page not found error".

```
<error-page>
    <error-code>404</error-code>
    <location>/errorCode.jsp</location>
</error-page>
```

c) To retrieve the exception object in JSP as below:

```
<%=
    request.getAttribute("javax.servlet.error.exception")
%>
```

d) The implicit object "exception" cannot be used for the global error/exception pages. Servlet exception package"javax.servlet.error.exception" is different from JSP exception package "javax.servlet.jsp.jspException"

214: How can we print stack trace of an exception in a JSP page?

Answer:

The stack trace of an exception in a JSP page can be printed as follows:

```
<%
```

```
if (exception != null) {
exception.printStackTrace(new PrintWriter(out));
}
%>
```

215: How can a JSP page be made thread safe in multithreaded environment?

Answer:

```
<%@ page isThreadSafe="false" %>
```

It will make the generated servlet implement the Single Thread Model interface. But this approach will reduce the performance of the page because of the overheads of instantiation and locking mechanism respectively. So we should take care of it before using synchronization.

216: What are the different types of directives available in JSP?

Answer:

The different types of directives available in JSP are:

a) **<@include>:** To include the content of another JSP file
b) **<@page>:** Used to handle thread safety, session, error page etc
c) **<@taglib>:** Used to declare custom tag library used in this page

217: Explain Page directives in JSP.

Answer:

Page directives define page attributes in the JSP file.

```
<% @ pagelanguage="Java" import="java.lang.*,java.util.*"
```

session="false" buffer="12KB" autoFlush="true"
errorPage="errorPage.jsp" %>

a) **import:** Imports Java packages into the JSP page. If the page requires a list of packages to be included, they can be a comma separated list

b) **session:** Specifies if the JSP page requires to be stored in a HTTP Session.

   session: "true": Session is available in this page. It can access the existing session or new session

   session: "false": Session is available for this page and implicit object session cannot be used

c) **buffer:** If buffer is not mentioned, output will be buffered to default buffer size. If buffer size is given as 40kb, the output will be buffered with this given buffer size.

d) **isThreadSafe:** Indicates if the JSP page is thread-safe or not

   isThreadSafe = "true": It is thread safe. One request will be processed at a time. It uses javax.servlet.SingleThreadModel interface in the servlet.

   isThreadSafe = "false": Not thread safe. Multiple requests will be sent to this JSP page at the same time by the JSP engine.

e) **errorPage:** It will redirect to another error page that is given as a URL in the errorPage attribute when runtime exception occurs

218: When do you use include directive and include action in JSP?

Answer:

a) **include directive:** <%@ include file="header.jsp" %>

b) **include action:** <jsp:include page="footer.jsp" flush="true" />

Include directive will add the included files' contents in the JSP translation phase. This does not impact performance.
Include action will add the contents of the included file at run time/during request processing time. This imposes extra performance overhead, and may take extra time to send the contents of the included page to client.

219: What is the default option of the session attribute in page directive and which is more efficient?

Answer:

<%@ page session="true|false" %>

The default option of the session attribute is true, meaning that a JSP page session will be created by the container/JSP. If a page does not require a session, the session should be set as false to reduce memory overhead and garbage collection, unnecessary creation of sessions, and to increase performance

220: How do we handle caching in a JSP page?

Answer:

Caching in a JSP page is handled with the following code:

```
<%
    response.setHeader("Pragma", "no-cache");
    response.setHeader("Cache-Control", "no-store");
    response.setDateHeader("Expires", 0);
%>
```

221: What are the differences between Application server and Webserver?

Answer:

The differences between an application server and a webserver are:

a) **Web Server:** Supports HTTP protocol. Features like Caching, Load balancing, and Clusters are not available in web server. It will handle a HTTP request and sends back the HTTP response to the web browser
b) **Application Server:** Supports HTTP/TCP/IP and more protocols. Caching, Load balancing, and Clusters are available here. It provides business logic to the client application programs through various protocols

222: How would you inform the browser not to cache the pages?

Answer:

The browser can be informed not to cache the pages with the following code:

```
public void doPost(HttpServletRequestreq,
HttpServletResponseresp) throws IOException,ServletException {
resp.setHeader("Cache-Control","no-cache"); // In HTTP 1.1
resp.setHeader("Pragma", "no-cache"); //HTTP 1.0
resp.setDateHeader("Expires", 0);
}
```

223: How would you implement caching in JSP?

Answer:

OSCache is an open source library used for page caching from OpenSymphony organization. It contains JSP tags that can be used for page caching in JSP applications. If the cache duration is 60 seconds, the page data will remain the same for all users who access before 60 seconds. After 60 seconds, it would display the fresh data.

a) **Cache entry**

   Cache entry is an object that is stored into a page cache. E.g. Output of a JSP page, part of a jsp page/servlet

b) **Cache key**

   When cache entry is stored in page cache it will be stored in a hashtable which will contain cache keys to identify the cache data. Cache keys such as URI, parameters like username and ipaddress are used to identify the cache data

c) **Cache duration**

   When a cache entry expires, it will be removed from page cache and will be regenerated again. Cache duration is the period of time that the cache entry remains in the page cache before it expires

d) **Cache scope**

   It defines the scope of the data. E.g. session or application

```
<%= newjava.util.Date().toString() %>
```

224: What are the caching mechanisms available for a JSP page to improve performance?

Answer:

The caching mechanisms available for a JSP page to improve performance are:

a) Using session and application implicit objects

b) Using application server caching
c) Using static and dynamic data in the JSP
d) Using third party caching algorithms

225: Explain the various caching techniques available for JSP.

Answer:

The various caching techniques available for JSP are:

a) **Using session and application implicit objects**
session.setAttribute() and session.getAttribute(), application.setAttribute() and application.getAttribute() methods are used for caching. The Session object is used for storing session data across multiple requests. The Application object is used for storing all users' data in the same application

b) **Using third party caching**
Open source third party caching algorithms can be used, for instance Opensymphony provides tags such as cach, usecached, and flush

c) **Using static data**
Caching in jspInit() method is used to cache static data which reduces its creation time. For caching dynamic data, you can write your own algorithm

d) **Application server caching**
Some application servers provide caching facilities and tags for caching dynamic data

226: How will you redirect one JSP to another resource (JSP/servlet)?

Answer:

One JSP can be redirected to another by using the send Redirect method of response object.

```
<% response.sendRedirect("http://www.google.com"); %>
(OR)
<% response.sendRedirect("target.jsp"); %>
```

227: What is the difference between <jsp:forward> and response.sendRedirect()?

Answer:

The difference between <jsp:forward> and response.sendRedirect() is that

a) **<jsp:forward>:** Transfers the control to another JSP/servlet/HTML file. Target should be within the same application context. Used to send errors to browsers

b) **sendRedirect:** Sends the control(URL) to the browser/client as a new request. Target file can be outside of current application. Used for sending client request to another JSP/servlet for processing

228: What is the main difference between SendRedirect and RequestDispatcher?

Answer:

The main difference between SendRedirect and RequestDispatcher is:

a) **SendRedirect:** Control will be redirected to client and new request will be carried over (Client side redirect)

b) **RequestDispatcher:** Control will be redirected to another JSP/servlet without the client's knowledge (Server side redirect)

229: Can we write database connection/jdbc code in JSP?

Answer:

Yes, we can write it in a scriptlet. But it is not a good practice. For better readability, we can try to avoid too much Java code in JSP.

```
<%
try{
    Class.forName("com.mysql.jdbc.Driver");
    Connection connection=
    DriverManager.getConnection("jdbc:mysql://localhost:3306/tes
    t", "root", "root");.
%>
```

230: In which of the servlet's lifecycle method would you prefer to create a database connection?

Answer:

The init() method is preferred to create a database connection. We can create a database connection as it is only called once when the container loads the servlet.

231: How would you create connections for many users?

Answer:

Connections for many users can be created using Connection pooling. We can create many connections and use it whenever they are required. It manages connections for many users and improves performance.

232: If you are retrieving data from a database and the result set have null values, how would the values be printed in the JSP input text fields?

Answer:

Null will be printed in the text fields if the values are null. We can update this value in JSP.

```
<%!
    String changeNull(String s) {
        return (s==null) ? \"\":s;
    }
%>
```

In JSP form,

```
<input type="text" name="fname"
value="<%=changeNull(fname)%>" />
```

233: If you set a request attribute in the JSP, will it be accessible in the subsequent servlet code?

Answer:

No, if we set a request in JSP, it would not be accessible in servlet since JSP file will be first translated into Servlet Java and executed on the server i.e. it is not in scope when it comes to subsequent servlet file/program.

However, if you set it in servlet then the subsequent JSP pages will be able to access it.

234: Can we set values for the parameters of the included JSP (jsp2) in the main JSP(jsp1)?

Answer:

Yes, we can set the value of included JSP in the main JSP as below. But it will not work if the setAttribute() is given after the include tag.

Main.JSP

```
<% request.setAttribute("userName ","ABC"); %>
<jsp:include page="includedFile.jsp" />
```

includedFile.jsp

```
<%= request.getAttribute("userName") %>
```

235: How would you pass information using request object from a servlet and forward it to a JSP? (or) explain how does a servlet communicate with a JSPpage.

Answer:

Information can be passed using request object from a servlet to a JSP as follows:

```
public class ServletDemo extends HttpServlet {
    public void doGet(HttpServletRequestreq,
    HttpServletResponseresp)  throws ServletException,
    IOException {
    String uname = "";
    req.setAttribute("uname", uname);
    List list = new ArrayList();
    list.add("uname");
    req.setAttribute("list", list);
    RequestDispatcherrd=
    getServletConfig().getServletContext().getRequestDispatcher("
    /jsp/loginProcess.jsp");
    rd.forward(req,resp);
}}
```

```
loginProcess.jsp:
<%
String uname = (String) request.getAttribute("uname ");
out.println("Username from the servlet: "+ uname);
List list = (List) request.getAttribute("list");
out.println("Object from the Servlet: "+ list.get(0));
%>
```

236: How would you synchronize the instance variables of a Servlet?

Answer:

Any servlet which implements SingleThreadModel interface will become thread safe. It does not require its instance variable to be explicitly synchronized. For example, we can declare Connection object as an instance variable.

```
public class TestServlet extends HttpServlet
implementsSingleThreadModel {
Connection con = null;// Synchronized
Public void init() { ... }
}
```

237: What is SingleThreadModel in a servlet?

Answer:

The SingleThreadModel interface is a marker interface that has no methods. A servlet that implements SingleThreadModel will execute one request at a time i.e. No two threads can concurrently execute the service() method of the servlet that implements the SingleThreadModel interface. Instance variables are thread safe in this approach but static variables and session attributes are not thread safe. So it is deprecated in Servlet API 2.4.

238: Provide an example of SingleThreadedModel in Servlets.

Answer:

A CreditCard Transaction is an example of SingleThreadedModel in Servlets. For every single user request, different threads are created and a copy of the servlet instances is shared among all requests.

239: Which is a better approach for enabling thread-safe servlets/JSP - Synchronization or SingleThreadModel?

Answer:

Synchronization is the better approach since SingleThreadModel does not resolve all kinds of thread safety issues.

a) If the servlet class implements SingleThreadModel interface, no two threads will access the servlet's service() method concurrently. Servlet engine guarantees thread safety by maintaining a pool of servlet instances and dispatching each concurrent request to a free servlet instance or by synchronizing the access to a single instance of the servlet

b) If more requests/concurrent requests come to the servlet, unprocessed requests should be queued until the resource is free which causes delays in processing. This is only suitable for small/low volume websites. Adding more memory or increasing the instance pool size cannot resolve it

c) SingleThreadModel does not guarantee all level of thread safety issues. For instance, it does not synchronize below attributes and they will be accessed by multiple threads/multiple requests at the same time
Instance variables
Static variables
Session attributes

d) Therefore, it is better to use explicit Synchronization for all shared data. However, it is advisable to minimize the use of synchronization to avoid other bottlenecks in multithreaded environment

240: What is RequestDispatcher in a servlet?

Answer:

In a servlet, RequestDispatcher forwards the control from one JSP/servlet to another. A servlet can do some logic for processing a request and it delegates the remaining work to another resource so as to generate a response to the client. It would forward the control to other resources or include other resources.

```
ServletContext sc = getServletContext();
RequestDispatcher rd =
sc.getRequestDispatcher("/targetServlet1");
rd.forward(req,resp); (or)
rd.include(req,resp);
```

Request >> Servlet1 (creates response) >> (**forward**) >> Servlet2 >> Response >> Client

Request >> Servlet1 (resp1) >> (**include**) >> Servlet2 (resp2) >> resp1+resp2 >> Client

(OR)

Request << Servlet1 << Servlet2

241: What is the difference between forward() and include() methods in RequestDispatcher?

Answer:

The differences between forward() and include() methods are:

a) **forward():** forward(ServletRequestreq, ServletResponseresp)

   It forwards the request to another JSP/servlet which will be responsible for sending the response to the client
   After a forward() call, print statement/other logic should not be written as the control will not return to the calling servlet. It will delegate the control to another resource

   ```
   rd.forward(req, res);
   ```

b) **include():** include(ServletRequestreq, ServletResponseresp)

   It includes the contents/response of another JSP/servlet within the calling servlet response
   After an include() call, other logic can be written, as the control will return to the calling servlet

   ```
   rd.include(req, res);
   ```

242: What is the difference between the getRequestDispatcher(String relPath) method of "ServletRequest" interface and the ServletContext interface?

Answer:

The differences between the getRequestDispatcher(String relPath) method of "ServletRequest" interface and the ServletContext interface are:

a) **ServletRequest:**

javax.servlet.ServletRequest package

```
RequestDispatcher rd =
request.getRequestDispatcher("/welcome.jsp");
```

It will dispatch (forward/include) the request relative to the current HTTPrequest. If path starts with "/", it is relative path

b) **ServletContext:**

javax.servlet.ServletContext package

```
RequestDispatcher rd =
getServletContext().getRequestDispatcher("/root/login.jsp"
);
```

It will dispatch (forward/include) the request relative to the root of the context

243: What is the difference between forward() of RequestDispatcher and response.sendRedirect() methods?

Answer:

The differences between forward() of RequestDispatcher and response.sendRedirect() methods are:

a) **forward():**
   i) Forwards the request to the next servlet/JSP within the server side without the client's knowledge
   ii) Need to provide relative path.

b) **sendRedirect():**
   i) Sends the header back to client browser which requires extra overhead/network trip
   ii) This header will contain the resource name to be redirected to

iii) The browser will send/process this header as a new request
iv) Need to provide absolute path of the resource
v) Used to bookmark the page
vi) Used to redirect to any resource in the same or different domain/application

244: Explain about ServletRequest interface.

Answer:

The ServletRequest interface can be explained as follows:

a) It handles the communication from client to server
b) It contains information such as parameters passed by the client to server, protocol used by the client, and remote host name from which the client requests reach the server
c) Servlets use the ServletInputStreaminterface to receive client information using POST and PUT methods
d) Interface that extends ServletRequest interface would retrieve more protocol specific data. E.g. HttpServletRequest

245: Explain about the ServletResponse interface.

Answer:

The ServletResponse interface can be explained as follows:

a) It handles the communication from the servlet back to the client
b) It contains information such as content length being set by servlet and MIME type of the reply
c) Servlets use the ServletOutputStream, a Writer through

which it can send data back to the client

d) Interface that extends ServletResponse interface would retrieve more protocol specific data. E.g. HttpServletResponse

246: How would you retrieve ServletConfig information defined in web.xml?

Answer:

The ServletConfig information defined in web.xml can be retrieved using getInitParameter() method. We can give it while overriding servlet's init() method.

```
publicvoid init() {
    ServletConfigsConfig=getServletConfig();
        String
        dbUsername=sConfig.getInitParameter("dbusername");
}
```

If init(ServletConfigconfig) is overridden, super.init(config) should be called explicitly.

247: How would you retrieve ServletConfig information given in web.xml when you may not know how many <init-param> are given or what is the param-name?

Answer:

Using getInitParameterNames() we can retrieve all config information given in web.xml and iterate through keys (param-name) and retrieve its values (param-value).

```
    public void init() {
        ServletConfig sc=getServletConfig();
Enumeration enum= sc.getInitParameterNames();
```

```
while(enum.hasMoreElements()) {
        String paramName= (String)enum.nextElement();
    String paramValue= getInitParameter(paramName);
}
```

248: How would you call a servlet along with parameters in the URL?

Answer:

The servlet could be called and the parameter name and value in the URL can be passed as a query string.

http://localhost:8080/servlet?param1=servlet1 | | param2=servlet2

249: What is servlet mapping?

Answer:

Servlet mapping is used by the web container to specify the servlet that should be invoked for the URL requested by the client. It is configured in web.xml and uses the <servlet-name>, <servlet-class> and <url-pattern> tags.

Client request >> web.xml >> (Map URL pattern and servlet class) >> Appropriate Servlet

250: What is Servlet mapping? How is it done in the web.xml?

Answer:

Servlet mapping is the technique used to map the corresponding java servlet against the web page requested. The servlet container has a repository of all servlet classes registered or compiled with the server. These have to be mapped against the page requested in the web.xml configuration file which resides in the WEB-INF directory. The code is as follows:

```
<servlet>
    <servlet-name>myLoginServlet</servlet-name>
    <servlet-class>myServer.myLoginServlet</servlet-class>
</servlet>
<servlet-mapping>
    <servlet-name>MyLoginServlet</servlet-name>
    <url-pattern>/MyLogin/*</url-pattern>
</servlet-mapping>
```

This is how the servlet mapping is configured/defined in the web.xml.

251: What is Servlet Invoker and how can it be enabled?

Answer:

Servlet Invoker is a mechanism provided by an earlier servlet container to call the servlet directly by servlet URL as "/loginServlet" without having to configure the servlet mapping in web.xml. For Instance, earlier Servlet Invoker option is enabled by default in Tomcat so the servlets placed inside /servlet/directory will be accessed by using the URL directly. Uncomment the below lines in the Tomcat's conf/web.xml file to enable the Servlet Invoker.

```
<!–
<servlet-mapping>
    <servlet-name>invokerServlet</servlet-name>
    <url-pattern>/servlet/*</url-pattern>
</servlet-mapping>
–>
```

```
<!–
<servlet>
    <servlet-name>invokerServlet</servlet-name>
    <servlet-
    class>org.apache.catalina.servlets.InvokerServlet</servlet-
    class>
    <init-param>
        <param-name>debug</param-name>
        <param-value>0</param-value>
    </init-param>
    <load-on-startup>1</load-on-startup>
</servlet>
–>
```

252: Why is the Servlet Invoker option disabled in the current version?

Answer:

The Servlet Invoker option is disabled in the current version because of the following reasons:

a) User would be able to access any servlet class that is inside a .jar or in classpath using its URL, which may cause a security risk. However, if we use web.xml configuration, the deployer would define which URL to be used
b) Class name would be displayed in the URL of client browsers. In web.xml configuration the URL can be defined and the class name hidden from the end user

253: What are the different ways available for session

persistence?

Answer:

The different ways available for session persistence are:

a) **Memory persistence (by default):**

   These are used in standalone application servers. Also, it can be used when two or more servers would like to share information. The application server is configured in such a way that any changes to session objects can be shared among all the servers so that the information will be available in multiple servers.

b) **Database:**

   All session objects will be persisted into the database so that all the application servers in the cluster would be able to share this session's contents from the database.

c) **Cookies:**

   These are unsecure and inefficient .It will store the session data in the client browser. Since the data is communicated between client and server, secure information like SSN cannot be stored in cookies and cookies can be disabled. If the data is not required to be stored in memory for small websites, we can use cookie persistence.

d) **File System:**

   The session objects/contents can be written in a file on the server and the location of the file is also configurable. All the servers in the cluster can use the contents. However, there will be a performance issue as it will cause some delay in reading from and writing to a file.

254: What is implicit mapping?

Answer:

Implicit mapping is done by the servlet container when the JSP and Servlet mappings are not provided in the web.xml file explicitly. JSP/Servlet mapping configured in the web.xml where mapping is done through URL patterns will have a higher precedence than the implicit mapping provided by the servlet container.

Implicit Servlet Mapping: Servlet container maps the URL pattern "/servlet" to the invoker servlet when the explicit servlet mappings are not provided in the web.xml file.

Server specific Invoker Servlet:

a) **Tomcat's:** "org.apache.catalina.servlets.InvokerServlet"
b) **JRun's:** "jrun.servlet.ServletInvoker"
c) **JBoss:** "org.apache.catalina.servlets.InvokerServlet"

Implicit JSP Mapping: Servlet container maps the "*.jsp" extension/URL pattern to the default JSP Servlet class "org.apache.jasper.servlet.JspServlet" which acts as a JSP page compiler and execution servlet.

Allows the JSP page to be executed on demand.

For Instance, below implicit JSP mappings can be found in the Tomcat's conf/web.xml file.

```
<servlet >
    <servlet-name>jsp</servlet-name>
    <servlet-
    class>org.apache.jasper.servlet.JspServlet</servlet-class>
</servlet >
<servlet-mapping>
```

```
    <servlet-name>jsp</servlet-name>
    <url-pattern>*.jsp</url-pattern>
  </servlet-mapping>
```

255: How would you handle I/O operations in JSP/Servlets?

Answer:

I/O operations in JSP/Servlets are handled with paths. Full path or relative path should be given for the files to retrieve them in JSP/servlets. We can retrieve the file path in two ways.

a) Files can be configured in web.xml using <init-param> tag. However, web.xml file should be changed if any changes in file path are made

```
<init-param>
    <param-name>config</param-name>
    <param-value>/WEB-INF/struts-config.xml</param-
    value>
</init-param>
```

b) We can place the files in the WEB-INF folder and access it using javax.servlet.ServletContext class and java.lang.ClassLoader class

```
InputStream
ins=config.getServletContext().getResourceAsStream("/use
r.xml");
```

256: What are the methods available to retrieve files placed in WEB-INF to JSP/servlets?

Answer:

The methods available to retrieve files placed in WEB-INF to JSP/servlets are:

a) InputStream is = config.getServletContext().getResourceAsStream("/user.xml");

b) Files placed inWEB-INF/classes directory

   URL url =

   config.getServletContext().getResource("/user.xml");

   BufferedReaderbuffReader = new BufferedReader(new InputStreamReader(url.openStream));

c) URL url = Thread.currentThread().getContextClassLoader().getResource("a.xml");

   BufferedWriterbufferedWriter= new BufferedWriter(new FileWriter(url.getFile());

257: What are the authentications available in Servlets?

Answer:

The authentications available in Servlets are:

a) **Basic Authentication:** The server will prompt for username and password when a client sends a request for any web resources. If username and password are wrong, it will prompt again for a fixed number of times. This authentication is not secure, as the password is not encrypted

b) **Digest Authentication:** Similar to basic authentication, but password is encrypted and password's hash value is transmitted

c) **Form-based Authentication:** Similar to basic authentication except a login will be displayed instead of a dialog, and an error page will be displayed if login fails

d) **SSL and Client Certificate Authentication:** Secure Sockets Layer (SSL) is a secured authentication mechanism and ensures privacy and data integrity through encryption. SSL details being added to a web server are server dependent. Client certificate authentication is implemented using SSL in which the client has to possess a public key certificate

258: How would you configure servlet authentication in web.xml?

Answer:

Servlet authentication in web.xml can be configured in the following methods:

a) Basic authentication:

```
<web-app>
    <security-constraint>
    <web-resource-collection>
        <web-resource-name>Secured Page</web-
        resource-name>
        <url-pattern>/account.jsp</url-pattern>
    </web-resource-collection>
    <auth-constraint>
        <role-name>admin</role-name>
        <role-name>role1</role-name>
        <role-name>role2</role-name>
    </auth-constraint>
    </security-constraint>
```

```
<login-config>
    <auth-method>BASIC</auth-method>
    <realm-name>BasicAuthentication</realm-name>
</login-config>
</web-app>
```

b) Digest authentication:

```
<login-config>
<auth-method>DIGEST</auth-method>
<realm-name>DigestAuthentication</realm-name>
</login-config>
```

c) Form-Based authentication:

```
<login-config>
<auth-method>FORM</auth-method>
<form-login-config>
    <form-login-page>/userLoginPage.jsp</form-login-
    page>
    <form-error-page>/errorPage.jsp</form-error-page>
</form-login-config>
</login-config>
```

259: How would you send user authentication information while creating a URL connection?

Answer:

User authentication information can be sent using HttpURLConnection.setRequestProperty() method while creating a URL connection, user basic authentication details such as username and password will be set.

```
URL url;
```

```
URLConnectionuconn;
String name="admin";
String pwd="admin";
try {
    url = new URL(URL);
    uconn = url.openConnection();
    if (name != null) {
    uconn.setRequestProperty("Authorization", "Basic " +
    encode(name + ":"+ pwd));
    }
}
```

260: How would you send a file to a browser from your application or download a file from the application?

Answer:

If the user clicks the file to download, it should invoke the servlet where the content type of the response and the Content-disposition for the response header would be set. The servlet would return the file data to the browser using ServletOutputStream and its write() method.Content-disposition of response header contains "attachment" which is used to invoke Save As dialog.

```
protectedvoiddoGet(HttpServletRequest request,
HttpServletResponse response) throwsServletException,
IOException{
ServletOutputStreamoutStream = response.getOutputStream();
String contentType = "application/x-download";
response.setContentType(contentType);
```

```
response.setHeader("Content-disposition", "attachment;filename="
+ downloadFileName+ "\"");
}
```

261: How would you send a file from the browser to application or upload a file to your application?

Answer:

If the user clicks the upload button, client will locate the local file that needs to be uploaded and send it to the servlet using the enctype as "multipart/form-data" and HTTP POST method. In this case the GET method is not secure. The file location can be configured in <context-param>. In the servlet, the doPost() method will have logic to extract the encoded file.

Test.JSP:

```
<formenctype="multipart/form-data" action="/testServlet"
method="POST">
```

Web.xml:

```
<context-param>
    <param-name>file-upload</param-name>
    <param-value>c:\apache-tomcat-5.5.29\webapps\data\
    </param-value>
</context-param>
```

262: What are the considerations for Servlet Clustering?

Answer:

The various considerations for Servlet Clustering are:

a) **Serializable object in session:** Objects that will be stored in session should be serializable

b) **Design for idempotence:** Servlet should be able to manage duplicate requests when the user clicks/send requests multiple times

c) **Avoid static and instance variables:** Should be avoided in write/read mode at distributed environments across JVMs. All states should be stored in an external resource (database)

d) **Avoid storing values ServletContext:** It is not serializable and many instances may be available in different JVMs

e) **Avoid using java.io.:** Files may not exist in all JVMs/machines. We can use getResourceAsStream() method instead

263: What is the difference between encodeURL and encodeRedirectURL?

Answer:

The differences between encodeURL and encodeRedirectURL are:

a) public String HttpServletResponse.encodeUrl(String encodeUrl)

Rewrites the specified URL to include the session id and returns the new URL. If cookies are already enabled, it won't change the URL, which is server specific. When the session id gets included into the empty URL string, this method converts it to an absolute URL by inserting session id

b) public StringHttpServletResponse.encodeRedirectUrl (String encodeUrl)

When the session id gets included into the empty URL string, this method does not convert the empty string by adding session id. The empty string will remain unchanged since session id is not inserted

264:What is URL Encoding and URL Decoding?

Answer:

a) **URL encoding:** All alphanumeric and special characters will remain the same. Spaces and other characters will be replaced with their hex characters. The Encode() method of URLEncoder class is used to encode the URL string

b) **URL decoding:** Replaces all hex characters with their original characters

265: How would you know if the http session is removed (when times out)?

Answer:

The class which needs to be stored in session objects should implement HttpSessionBindingListener interface (javax.servlet.http package) and override valueUnbound() and valueBound() methods to know if the http session is removed. If the session is timed out or removed, the servlet container will invoke the valueUnbound() method on the class object. If this class object is stored into the session for the next user valueBound() method will be invoked.

HttpSessionBindingListener interfaced is used to track the session events on the particular object.

public void valueBound(HttpSessionBindingEventboundEvent)

public void valueUnbound(HttpSessionBindingEventunboundEvent)

266: How do we set query and database driver details in JSP using JSTL?

Answer:

Query and database driver details in JSP are set using JSTL as follows:

a) Define the sql uri and prefix attributes of the taglib in the JSP page
b) Using <sql:setDataSource> tag give the dataS source details in the driver, URL, user, and password attributes
c) Write the sql query within <sql:query> and </sql:query> tags by passing the dataSource variable which has been set in step (b), in the data source attribute
d) We can iterate this result set by iterating the variable set in <sql:query> tag, using <c:forEach> tag

267: What is internationalization (I18N) and locale?

Answer:

Internationalization is enabling a website having different versions of content translated. Locale is a representation of language code underscore(_) country code. E.g. en_US.

268: How would you detect Locale in a JSP page?

Answer:

Locale can be detected in a JSP page by:

a) Getting client locale using getLocale() method of request object and store it in Locale object

    Locale loc = request.getLocale().

b) Getting language code and country code by invoking

getCountry() and getLanguage() on locale object

loc.getCountry(); and loc.getLanguage();

269: Describe EL and what it can be used for.

Answer:

EL stands for Expression Language and is used to access application data. i.e. it is used to represent the variable value. E.g. Username is ${uname}

270: In which order does EL search for an attribute?

Answer:

EL will search for an attribute in the scope object as below: Firstly, it will search whether the attribute is available in page scope; if not, it will check in request object, then session and finally application.

If it doesn't find any match it would display an empty string.

E.g. Username: ${uname}will display "Username: "

271: How would you disable EL in JSP?

Answer:

We would be able to enable/disable EL using the isELIgnored attribute of page directive in the JSP.

<%@ pageisELIgnored ="true|false" %>

272: What implicit EL objects are available in JSP?

Answer:

The implicit EL objects available in JSP are:

a) **PageContext:** Contains the object's reference, such as servletContext, session, request, and response

b) **Param:** Indicates the request parameter name
c) **paramValues:** Maps the request parameter name to the array of values
d) **Header:** Indicates the request header
e) **Cookie:** Maps the cookie name to a single cookie
f) **initParam:** Indicates the initialization context parameter name

273: Why do we need a thread pool for the JSP engine?

Answer:

JSP engine creates a separate thread for every new client request and assigns that thread to _jspService() method in its multithreaded JSP servlet. Finally, it removes that thread after the completion of _jspService() method execution. This reduces performance since creating and removing threads is expensive. It can be avoided using a thread pool.

JSP engine will create a pool of threads at startup and assign these threads to each request instead of creating new threads at the time of request processing. Once _jspService() method execution completes it will return that thread to the pool.

The thread pool's default size is configured in the JSP engine's configuration file. The minimum and maximum number of threads in the pool can be defined. We need to estimate the number of concurrent users and set the pool size accordingly. Tomcat's JSP engine provides a facility to define thread pool size.

274: What do you mean by Connection Pooling?

Answer:

Connection pooling provides a cache of database connections that can be used whenever required. When the application server starts, it creates a number of connection objects, which are placed in a pool for later use. The number of connections such as 10, 20, and 50 depends upon database size and how it is configured in the container. When an application requires a connection it will retrieve it from the pool and then return it after using it.

275: Can we use ServletOutputStream object from JSP?

Answer:

No. JspWriter needs to be used in the form of an implicit object (out) when sending data to client. ServletOutputStream is for sending binary data to client. JspWriter is the buffered version of the stream object. If the page is not buffered, output written into a JspWriter object will be directly written to PrintWriter. If the page is buffered, PrintWriter object will not be created until the buffer is flushed. We can disable the buffer option for a JSP page as below.

```
<%@ page buffer="none" %>
```

276: What is the use of <load-on-startup> tag in web.xml?

Answer:

By default the servlet container would not initialize the servlet when the server is started. It will initialize it when it receives a request for that servlet for the first time. It is called lazy loading. If we define the <load-on-startup> tag, the container will load and initialize the servlet when the server is started. This is called Pre-

Initialization of Servlet or preloading. The 'load-on-startup' tag value should be non-zero/positive.

<load-on-startup>1</load-on-startup>

This is the use of <load-on-startup> tag in web.xml.

277: What is a deployment descriptor?

Answer:

A deployment descriptor in a web application is the XML configuration file where we can map URL with the servlets, provide authorization for URLs, and configure listeners and other information. It will provide a loosely coupled environment which will separate business logic and configuration files. In a Java web application, the deployment descriptor is web.xml which will be in WEB-INF/web.xml.

278: How will you retrieve the multiple init parameters of a servlet defined in web.xml?

Answer:

The multiple init parameters of a servlet defined in web.xml can be retrieved by the following steps:

a) Define multiple init parameters for a servlet in web.xml
b) Using getInitParameterNames() method, all the <init-param> initialization parameters can be retrieved. This will return Enumeration of the initialization parameters
c) Using the hasMoreElements() method of Enumeration class, init parameters can be iterated

279: The remote server details such as name and IP are given in <init-param> tag (web.xml) and the connection is being done in a servlet called ConnServlet.java. If I move all the data to another server, what are the changes that need to be done?

Answer:

If we move all the data to another server, the following changes are to be done:

a) Name and IP of the new server should be changed in <init-param> tag (web.xml)
b) Restart the server since the web.xml file is changed

280: Explain session migration.

Answer:

Session migration refers to moving the session from one server to another (in a distributed environment) in case of any failure, to preserve the session data. Session migration can be achieved by:

a) Persisting session data into database
b) Storing it in memory on multiple servers, which can be used across the network. If anything happens in one server, session data can be shared from other servers as well

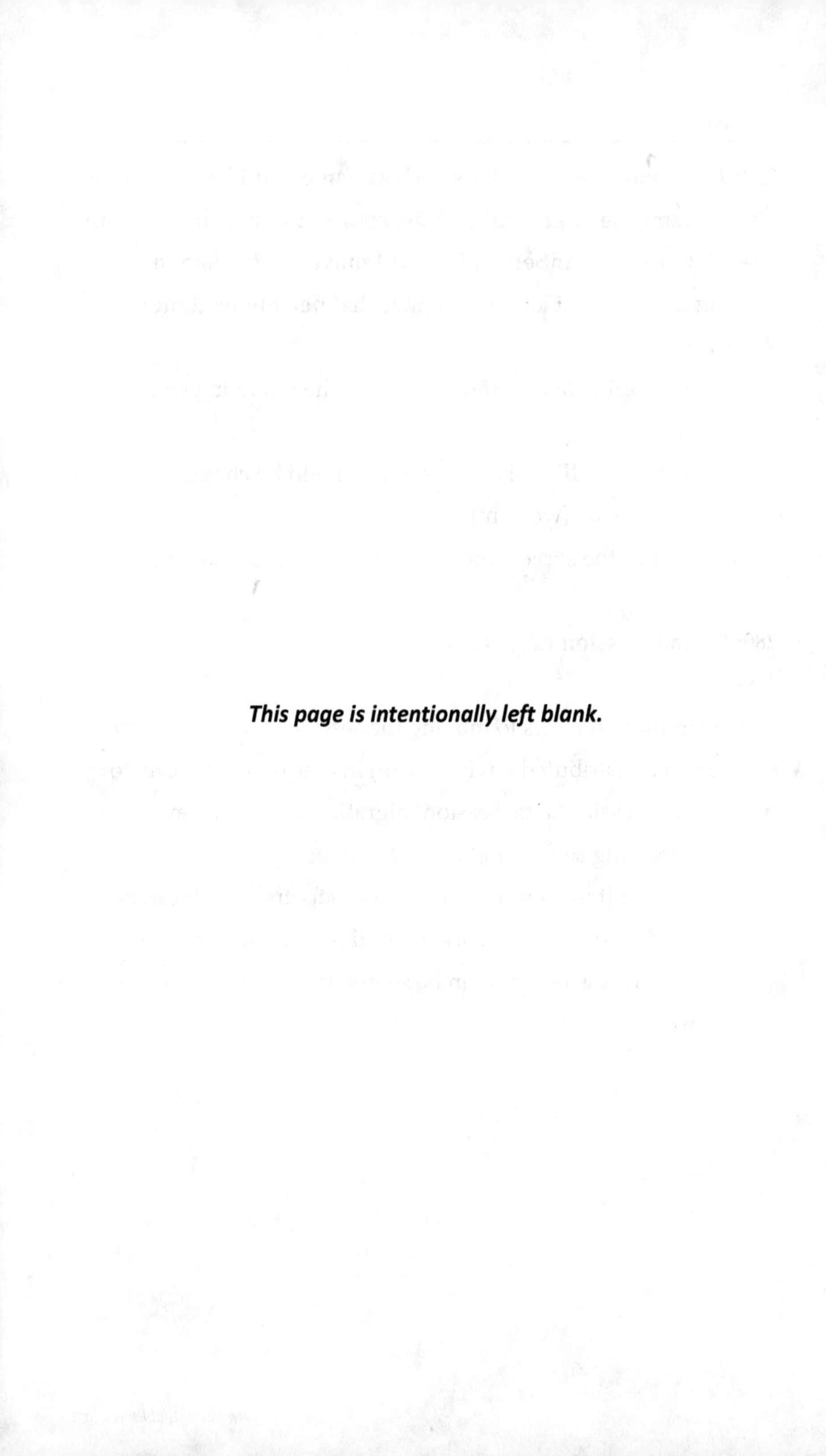

This page is intentionally left blank.

HR Questions

Review these typical interview questions and think about how you would answer them. Read the answers listed; you will find best possible answers along with strategies and suggestions.

1: Where do you find ideas?

Answer:

Ideas can come from all places, and an interviewer wants to see that your ideas are just as varied. Mention multiple places that you gain ideas from, or settings in which you find yourself brainstorming. Additionally, elaborate on how you record ideas or expand upon them later.

2: How do you achieve creativity in the workplace?

Answer:

It's important to show the interviewer that you're capable of being resourceful and innovative in the workplace, without stepping outside the lines of company values. Explain where ideas normally stem from for you (examples may include an exercise such as list-making or a mind map), and connect this to a particular task in your job that it would be helpful to be creative in.

3: How do you push others to create ideas?

Answer:

If you're in a supervisory position, this may be requiring employees to submit a particular number of ideas, or to complete regular idea-generating exercises, in order to work their creative muscles. However, you can also push others around you to create ideas simply by creating more of your own. Additionally, discuss with the interviewer the importance of questioning people as a way to inspire ideas and change.

4: Describe your creativity.

Answer:

Try to keep this answer within the professional realm, but if you have an impressive background in something creative outside of your employment history, don't be afraid to include it in your answer also. The best answers about creativity will relate problem-solving skills, goal-setting, and finding innovative ways to tackle a project or make a sale in the workplace. However, passions outside of the office are great, too (so long as they don't cut into your work time or mental space).

5: Would you rather receive more authority or more responsibility at work?

Answer:

There are pros and cons to each of these options, and your interviewer will be more interested to see that you can provide a critical answer to the question. Receiving more authority may mean greater decision-making power and may be great for those with outstanding leadership skills, while greater responsibility may be a growth opportunity for those looking to advance steadily throughout their careers.

6: What do you do when someone in a group isn't contributing their fair share?

Answer:

This is a particularly important question if you're interviewing for a position in a supervisory role – explain the ways in which you would identify the problem, and how you would go about pulling aside the individual to discuss their contributions. It's important to understand the process of creating a dialogue, so that you can communicate your expectations clearly to the individual, give them a chance to respond, and to make clear what needs to change. After this, create an action plan with the group member to ensure their contributions are on par with others in the group.

7: Tell me about a time when you made a decision that was outside of your authority.

Answer:

While an answer to this question may portray you as being decisive and confident, it could also identify you to an employer as a potential problem employee. Instead, it may be best to slightly refocus the question into an example of a time that you took on additional responsibilities, and thus had to make decisions that were outside of your normal authority (but which had been granted to you in the specific instance). Discuss how the weight of the decision affected your decision-making process, and the outcomes of the situation.

8: Are you comfortable going to supervisors with disputes?

Answer:

If a problem arises, employers want to know that you will handle it in a timely and appropriate manner. Emphasize that you've rarely had disputes with supervisors in the past, but if a situation were to arise, you feel perfectly comfortable in discussing it with the person in question in order to find a resolution that is satisfactory to both parties.

9: If you had been in charge at your last job, what would you have done differently?

Answer:

No matter how many ideas you have about how things could run better, or opinions on the management at your previous job, remain positive when answering this question. It's okay to show thoughtful reflection on how something could be handled in order to increase efficiency or improve sales, but be sure to keep all of your suggestions focused on making things better, rather than talking about ways to eliminate waste or negativity.

10: Do you believe employers should praise or reward employees for a job well done?

Answer:

Recognition is always great after completing a difficult job, but there are many employers who may ask this question as a way to infer as to whether or not you'll be a high-maintenance worker. While you may appreciate rewards or praise, it's important to convey to the interviewer that you don't require accolades to be confident that you've done your job well. If you are interviewing for a supervisory position where you would be the one praising other employees, highlight the importance of praise in boosting team morale.

11: What do you believe is the most important quality a leader can have?

Answer:

There are many important skills for a leader to have in any

business, and the most important component of this question is that you explain why the quality you choose to highlight is important. Try to choose a quality such as communication skills, or an ability to inspire people, and relate it to a specific instance in which you displayed the quality among a team of people.

12: Tell me about a time when an unforeseen problem arose. How did you handle it?

Answer:

It's important that you are resourceful, and level-headed under pressure. An interviewer wants to see that you handle problems systematically, and that you can deal with change in an orderly process. Outline the situation clearly, including all solutions and results of the process you implemented.

13: Can you give me an example of a time when you were able to improve *X objective* at your previous job?

Answer:

It's important here to focus on an improvement you made that created tangible results for your company. Increasing efficiency is certainly a very important element in business, but employers are also looking for concrete results such as increased sales or cut expenses. Explain your process thoroughly, offering specific numbers and evidence wherever possible, particularly in outlining the results.

14: Tell me about a time when a supervisor did not provide specific enough direction on a project.

Answer:

While many employers want their employees to follow very specific guidelines without much decision-making power, it's important also to be able to pick up a project with vague direction and to perform self-sufficiently. Give examples of necessary questions that you asked, and specify how you determined whether a question was something you needed to ask of a supervisor or whether it was something you could determine on your own.

15: Tell me about a time when you were in charge of leading a project.

Answer:

Lead the interviewer through the process of the project, just as you would have with any of your team members. Explain the goal of the project, the necessary steps, and how you delegated tasks to your team. Include the results, and what you learned as a result of the leadership opportunity.

16: Tell me about a suggestion you made to a former employer that was later implemented.

Answer:

Employers want to see that you're interested in improving your company and doing your part – offer a specific example of something you did to create a positive change in your previous job. Explain how you thought of the idea, how your supervisors received it, and what other employees thought was the idea was put into place.

17: Tell me about a time when you thought of a way something in the workplace could be done more efficiently.

Answer:

Focus on the positive aspects of your idea. It's important not to portray your old company or boss negatively, so don't elaborate on how inefficient a particular system was. Rather, explain a situation in which you saw an opportunity to increase productivity or to streamline a process, and explain in a general step-by-step how you implemented a better system.

18: Is there a difference between leading and managing people – which is your greater strength?

Answer:

There is a difference – leaders are often great idea people, passionate, charismatic, and with the ability to organize and inspire others, while managers are those who ensure a system runs, facilitate its operations, make authoritative decisions, and who take great responsibility for all aspects from overall success to the finest decisions. Consider which of these is most applicable to the position, and explain how you fit into this role, offering concrete examples of your past experience.

19: Do you function better in a leadership role, or as a worker on a team?

Answer:

It is important to consider what qualities the interviewer is looking for in your position, and to express how you embody this role. If you're a leader, highlight your great ideas, drive and passion, and ability to incite others around you to action. If you work great in teams, focus on your dedication to the task at hand, your cooperation and communication skills, and your ability to keep things

20: Tell me about a time when you discovered something in the workplace that was disrupting your (or others) productivity – what did you do about it?

Answer:

Try to not focus on negative aspects of your previous job too much, but instead choose an instance in which you found a positive, and quick, solution to increase productivity. Focus on the way you noticed the opportunity, how you presented a solution to your supervisor, and then how the change was implemented (most importantly, talk about how you led the change initiative). This is a great opportunity for you to display your problem-solving skills, as well as your resourceful nature and leadership skills.

21: How do you perform in a job with clearly-defined objectives and goals?

Answer:

It is important to consider the position when answering this question – clearly, it is best if you can excel in a job with clearly-defined objectives and goals (particularly if you're in an entry level or sales position). However, if you're applying for a position with a leadership role or creative aspect to it, be sure to focus on the ways that you additionally enjoy the challenges of developing and implementing your own ideas.

22: How do you perform in a job where you have great decision-making power?

Answer:

The interviewer wants to know that, if hired, you won't be the type of employee who needs constant supervision or who asks for advice, authority, or feedback every step of the way. Explain that you work well in a decisive, productive environment, and that you look forward to taking initiative in your position.

23: If you saw another employee doing something dishonest or unethical, what would you do?

Answer:

In the case of witnessing another employee doing something dishonest, it is always best to act in accordance with company policies for such a situation – and if you don't know what this company's specific policies are, feel free to simply state that you would handle it according to the policy and by reporting it to the appropriate persons in charge. If you are aware of the company's policies (such as if you are seeking a promotion within your own company), it is best to specifically outline your actions according to the policy.

24: Tell me about a time when you learned something on your own that later helped in your professional life.

Answer:

This question is important because it allows the interviewer to gain insight into your dedication to learning and advancement. Choose an example solely from your personal life, and provide a brief anecdote ending in the lesson you learned. Then, explain in a clear and thorough manner how this lesson has translated into a usable skill or practice in your position.

25: Tell me about a time when you developed a project idea at work.

Answer:

Choose a project idea that you developed that was typical of projects you might complete in the new position. Outline where your idea came from, the type of research you did to ensure its success and relevancy, steps that were included in the project, and the end results. Offer specific before and after statistics, to show its success.

26: Tell me about a time when you took a risk on a project.

Answer:

Whether the risk involved something as complex as taking on a major project with limited resources or time, or simply volunteering for a task that was outside your field of experience, show that you are willing to stretch out of your comfort zone and to try new things. Offer specific examples of why something you did was risky, and explain what you learned in the process – or how this prepared you for a job objective you later faced in your career.

27: What would you tell someone who was looking to get into

this field?

Answer:

This question allows you to be the expert – and will show the interviewer that you have the knowledge and experience to go along with any training and education on your resume. Offer your knowledge as advice of unexpected things that someone entering the field may encounter, and be sure to end with positive advice such as the passion or dedication to the work that is required to truly succeed.

28: Tell me about a time when you worked additional hours to finish a project.

Answer:

It's important for your employer to see that you are dedicated to your work, and willing to put in extra hours when required or when a job calls for it. However, be careful when explaining why you were called to work additional hours – for instance, did you have to stay late because you set goals poorly earlier in the process? Or on a more positive note, were you working additional hours because a client requested for a deadline to be moved up on short notice? Stress your competence and willingness to give 110% every time.

29: Tell me about a time when your performance exceeded the duties and requirements of your job.

Answer:

If you're a great candidate for the position, this should be an easy question to answer – choose a time when you truly went above and beyond the call of duty, and put in additional work or voluntarily took on new responsib-ilities. Remain humble, and express gratitude for the learning opportunity, as well as confidence in your ability to give a repeat performance.

30: What is your driving attitude about work?

Answer:

There are many possible good answers to this question, and the interviewer primarily wants to see that you have a great passion for the job and that you will remain motivated in your career if hired. Some specific driving forces behind your success may include hard work, opportunity, growth potential, or success.

31: Do you take work home with you?

Answer:

It is important to first clarify that you are always willing to take work home when necessary, but you want to emphasize as well that it has not been an issue for you in the past. Highlight skills such as time management, goal-setting, and multi-tasking, which can all ensure that work is completed at work.

32: Describe a typical work day to me.

Answer:

There are several important components in your typical work day, and an interviewer may derive meaning from any or all of them, as well as from your ability to systematically lead him or her through the day. Start at the beginning of your day and proceed chronologically, making sure to emphasize steady productivity, time for review, goal-setting, and prioritizing, as well as some additional time to account for unexpected things that may arise.

33: Tell me about a time when you went out of your way at your previous job.

Answer:

Here it is best to use a specific example of the situation that required you to go out of your way, what your specific position would have required that you did, and how you went above that. Use concrete details, and be sure to include the results, as well as reflection on what you learned in the process.

34: Are you open to receiving feedback and criticisms on your job performance, and adjusting as necessary?

Answer:

This question has a pretty clear answer – yes – but you'll need to display a knowledge as to why this is important. Receiving feedback and criticism is one thing, but the most important part of that process is to then implement it into your daily work. Keep a good attitude, and express that you always appreciate constructive feedback.

35: What inspires you?

Answer:

You may find inspiration in nature, reading success stories, or mastering a difficult task, but it's important that your inspiration is positively-based and that you're able to listen and tune into it when it appears. Keep this answer generally based in the professional world, but where applicable, it may stretch a bit into creative exercises in your personal life that, in turn, help you in achieving career objectives.

36: How do you inspire others?

Answer:

This may be a difficult question, as it is often hard to discern the effects of inspiration in others. Instead of offering a specific example of a time when you inspired someone, focus on general principles such as leading by example that you employ in your professional life. If possible, relate this to a quality that someone who inspired you possessed, and discuss the way you have modified or modeled it in your own work.

37: How do you make decisions?

Answer:

This is a great opportunity for you to wow your interviewer with your decisiveness, confidence, and organizational skills. Make sure that you outline a process for decision-making, and that you stress the importance of weighing your options, as well as in trusting intuition. If you answer this question skillfully and with ease, your interviewer will trust in your capability as a worker.

38: What are the most difficult decisions for you to make?

Answer:

Explain your relationship to decision-making, and a general synopsis of the process you take in making choices. If there is a particular type of decision that you often struggle with, such as those that involve other people, make sure to explain why that type of decision is tough for you, and how you are currently engaged in improving your skills.

39: When making a tough decision, how do you gather information?

Answer:

If you're making a tough choice, it's best to gather information from as many sources as possible. Lead the interviewer through your process of taking information from people in different areas, starting first with advice from experts in your field, feedback from coworkers or other clients, and by looking analytically at your own past experiences.

40: Tell me about a decision you made that did not turn out well.

Answer:

Honesty and transparency are great values that your interviewer will appreciate – outline the choice you made, why you made it, the results of your poor decision – and finally (and most importantly!) what you learned from the decision. Give the interviewer reason to trust that you wouldn't make a decision like that again in the future.

41: Are you able to make decisions quickly?

Answer:

You may be able to make decisions quickly, but be sure to communicate your skill in making sound, thorough decisions as well. Discuss the importance of making a decision quickly, and how you do so, as well as the necessity for each decision to first be well-informed.

42: Ten years ago, what were your career goals?

Answer:

In reflecting back to what your career goals were ten years ago, it's important to show the ways in which you've made progress in that time. Draw distinct links between specific objectives that you've achieved, and speak candidly about how it felt to reach those goals. Remain positive, upbeat, and growth-oriented, even if you haven't yet achieved all of the goals you set out to reach.

43: Tell me about a weakness you used to have, and how you changed it.

Answer:

Choose a non-professional weakness that you used to have, and outline the process you went through in order to grow past it. Explain the weakness itself, why it was problematic, the action steps you planned, how you achieved them, and the end result.

44: Tell me about your goal-setting process.

Answer:

When describing your goal-setting process, clearly outline the way that you create an outline for yourself. It may be helpful to offer an example of a particular goal you've set in the past, and use this as a starting point to guide the way you created action steps, check-in points, and how the goal was eventually achieved.

45: Tell me about a time when you solved a problem by creating actionable steps to follow.

Answer:

This question will help the interviewer to see how you talented you are in outlining, problem resolution, and goal-setting. Explain thoroughly the procedure of outlining the problem, establishing steps to take, and then how you followed the steps (such as through check-in points along the way, or intermediary goals).

46: Where do you see yourself five years from now?

Answer:

Have some idea of where you would like to have advanced to in the position you're applying for, over the next several years. Make sure that your future plans line up with you still working for the company, and stay positive about potential advancement. Focus on future opportunities, and what you're looking forward to – but make sure your reasons for advancement are admirable, such as greater experience and the chance to learn, rather than simply being out for a higher salary.

47: When in a position, do you look for opportunities to promote?

Answer:

There's a fine balance in this question – you want to show the interviewer that you have initiative and motivation to advance in your career, but not at the expense of appearing opportunistic or selfishly-motivated. Explain that you are always open to growth opportunities, and very willing to take on new responsibilities as your career advances.

48: On a scale of 1 to 10, how successful has your life been?

Answer:

Though you may still have a long list of goals to achieve, it's important to keep this answer positively-focused. Choose a high number between 7 and 9, and explain that you feel your life has been largely successful and satisfactory as a result of several specific achievements or experiences. Don't go as high as a 10, as the interviewer may not believe your response or in your ability to reason critically.

49: What is your greatest goal in life?

Answer:

It's okay for this answer to stray a bit into your personal life, but best if you can keep it professionally-focused. While specific goals are great, if your personal goal doesn't match up exactly with one of the company's objectives, you're better off keeping your goal a little more generic and encompassing, such as "success in my career" or "leading a happy and fulfilling life." Keep your answer brief, and show a decisive nature – most importantly, make it clear that you've already thought about this question and know what you want.

50: Tell me about a time when you set a goal in your personal life and achieved it.

Answer:

The interviewer can see that you excel at setting goals in your professional life, but he or she also wants to know that you are consistent in your life and capable of setting goals outside of the office as well. Use an example such as making a goal to eat more healthily or to drink more water, and discuss what steps you outlined to achieve your goal, the process of taking action, and the final results as well.

51: What is your greatest goal in your career?

Answer:

Have a very specific goal of something you want to achieve in your career in mind, and be sure that it's something the position clearly puts you in line to accomplish. Offer the goal as well as your plans to get there, and emphasize clear ways in which this position will be an opportunity to work toward the goal.

52: Tell me about a time when you achieved a goal.

Answer:

Start out with how you set the goal, and why you chose it. Then, take the interviewer through the process of outlining the goal, taking steps to achieve it, the outcome, and finally, how you felt after achieving it or recognition you received. The most important part of this question includes the planning and implementation of strategies, so focus most of your time on explaining these aspects. However, the preliminary decisions and end results are also important, so make sure to include them as well.

53: What areas of your work would you still like to improve in?

What are your plans to do this?

Answer:

While you may not want the interviewer to focus on things you could improve on, it's important to be self-aware of your own growth opportunities. More importantly, you can impress an interviewer by having specific goals and actions outlined in order to facilitate your growth, even if your area of improvement is something as simple as increasing sales or finding new ways to create greater efficiency.

54: Tell me about your favorite book or newspaper.

Answer:

The interviewer will look at your answer to this question in order to determine your ability to analyze and review critically. Additionally, try to choose something that is on a topic related to your field or that embodies a theme important to your work, and be able to explain how it relates. Stay away from controversial subject matter, such as politics or religion.

55: If you could be rich or famous, which would you choose?

Answer:

This question speaks to your ability to think creatively, but your answer may also give great insight to your character. If you answer rich, your interviewer may interpret that you are self-confident and don't seek approval from others, and that you like to be rewarded for your work. If you choose famous, your interviewer may gather that you like to be well-known and to deal with people, and to have the platform to deliver your message to others. Either way, it's important to back up your answer with sound reasoning.

56: If you could trade places with anyone for a week, who would it be and why?

Answer:

This question is largely designed to test your ability to think on your feet, and to come up with a reasonable answer to an outside the box question. Whoever you choose, explain your answer in a logical manner, and offer specific professional reasons that led you to choose the individual.

57: What would you say if I told you that just from glancing over your resume, I can already see three spelling mistakes?

Answer:

Clearly, your resume should be absolutely spotless – and you should be confident that it is. If your interviewer tries to make you second-guess yourself here, remain calm and poised and assert with a polite smile that you would be quite surprised as you are positive that your resume is error-free.

58: Tell me about your worldview.

Answer:

This question is designed to offer insight into your personality, so be aware of how the interviewer will interpret your answer. Speak openly and directly, and try to incorporate your own job skills into your outlook on life. For example, discuss your beliefs on the ways that hard work and dedication can always bring success, or in how learning new things is one of life's greatest gifts. It's okay to expand into general life principles here, but try to keep your thoughts related to the professional field as well.

59: What is the biggest mistake someone could make in an interview?

Answer:

The biggest mistake that could be made in an interview is to be caught off guard! Make sure that you don't commit whatever you answer here, and additionally be prepared for all questions. Other common mistakes include asking too early in the hiring process about job benefits, not having questions prepared when the interviewer asks if you have questions, arriving late, dressing casually or sloppily, or showing ignorance of the position.

60: If you won the $50m lottery, what would you do with the money?

Answer:

While a question such as this may seem out of place in a job interview, it's important to display your creative thinking and your ability to think on the spot. It's also helpful if you choose something admirable, yet believable, to do with the money such as donate the first seventy percent to a charitable cause, and divide the remainder among gifts for friends, family, and of course, yourself.

61: Is there ever a time when honesty isn't appropriate in the workplace?

Answer:

This may be a difficult question, but the only time that honesty isn't appropriate in the workplace is perhaps when you're feeling anger or another emotion that is best kept to yourself. If this is the case, explain simply that it is best to put some thoughts aside, and clarify that the process of keeping some thoughts quiet is often enough to smooth over any unsettled emotions, thus eliminating the problem.

62: If you could travel anywhere in the world, where would it be?

Answer:

This question is meant to allow you to be creative – so go ahead and stretch your thoughts to come up with a unique answer. However, be sure to keep your answer professionally-minded. For example, choose somewhere rich with culture or that would expose you to a new experience, rather than going on an expensive cruise through the Bahamas.

63: What would I find in your refrigerator right now?

Answer:

An interviewer may ask a creative question such as this in order to discern your ability to answer unexpected questions calmly, or, to try to gain some insight into your personality. For example, candidates with a refrigerator full of junk food or take-out may be more likely to be under stress or have health issues, while a candidate with a balanced refrigerator full of nutritious staples may be more likely to lead a balanced mental life, as well.

64: If you could play any sport professionally, what would it be and what aspect draws you to it?

Answer:

Even if you don't know much about professional sports, this question might be a great opportunity to highlight some of your greatest professional working skills. For example, you may choose to play professional basketball, because you admire the teamwork and coordination that goes into creating a solid play. Or, you may choose to play professional tennis, because you consider yourself to be a go-getter with a solid work ethic and great dedication to perfecting your craft. Explain your choice simply to the interviewer without elaborating on drawn-out sports metaphors, and be sure to point out specific areas or skills in which you excel.

65: Who were the presidential and vice-presidential candidates in the 2008 elections?

Answer:

This question, plain and simple, is intended as a gauge of your intelligence and awareness. If you miss this question, you may well fail the interview. Offer your response with a polite smile, because you understand that there are some individuals who probably miss this question.

66: Explain X task in a few short sentences as you would to a second-grader.

Answer:

An interviewer may ask you to break down a normal job task that you would complete in a manner that a child could understand, in part to test your knowledge of the task's inner workings – but in larger part, to test your ability to explain a process in simple, basic terms. While you and your coworkers may be able to converse using highly technical language, being able to simplify a process is an important skill for any employee to have.

67: If you could compare yourself to any animal, what would it be?

Answer:

Many interviewers ask this question, and it's not to determine which character traits you think you embody – instead, the interviewer wants to see that you can think outside the box, and that you're able to reason your way through any situation. Regardless of what animal you answer, be sure that you provide a thorough reason for your choice.

68: Who is your hero?

Answer:

Your hero may be your mother or father, an old professor,– but keep your reasoning for your choice professional, and be prepared to offer a logical train of thought. Choose someone who embodies values that are important in your chosen career field, and answer the question with a smile and sense of passion.

69: Who would play you in the movie about your life?

Answer:

As with many creative questions that challenge an interviewee to think outside the box, the answer to this question is not as important as how you answer it. Choose a professional, and relatively non-controversial actor or actress, and then be prepared to offer specific reasoning for your choice, employing important skills or traits you possess.

70: Name five people, alive or dead, that would be at your ideal dinner party.

Answer:

Smile and sound excited at the opportunity to think outside the box when asked this question, even if it seems to come from left field. Choose dynamic, inspiring individuals who you could truly learn from, and explain what each of them would have to offer to the conversation. Don't forget to include yourself, and to talk about what you would bring to the conversation as well!

71: What is customer service?

Answer:

Customer service can be many things – and the most important consideration in this question is that you have a creative answer. Demonstrate your ability to think outside the box by offering a confident answer that goes past a basic definition, and that shows you have truly considered your own individual view of what it means to take care of your customers. The thoughtful consideration you hold for customers will speak for itself.

72: Tell me about a time when you went out of your way for a customer.

Answer:

It's important that you offer an example of a time you truly went out of your way – be careful not to confuse something that felt like a big effort on your part, with something your employer would expect you to do anyway. Offer an example of the customer's problems, what you did to solve it, and the way the customer responded after you took care of the situation.

73: How do you gain confidence from customers?

Answer:

This is a very open-ended question that allows you to show your customer service skills to the interviewer. There are many possible answers, and it is best to choose something that you've had great experience with, such as "by handling situations with transparency," "offering rewards," or "focusing on great communication." Offer specific examples of successes you've had.

74: Tell me about a time when a customer was upset or agitated – how did you handle the situation?

Answer:

Similarly to handling a dispute with another employee, the most important part to answering this question is to first set up the scenario, offer a step-by-step guide to your particular conflict resolution style, and end by describing the way the conflict was resolved. Be sure that in answering questions about your own conflict resolution style, that you emphasize the importance of open communication and understanding from both parties, as well as a willingness to reach a compromise or other solution.

75: When can you make an exception for a customer?

Answer:

Exceptions for customers can generally be made when in accordance with company policy or when directed by a supervisor. Display an understanding of the types of situations in which an exception should be considered, such as when a customer has endured a particular hardship, had a complication with an order, or at a request.

76: What would you do in a situation where you were needed by both a customer and your boss?

Answer:

While both your customer and your boss have different needs of you and are very important to your success as a worker, it is always best to try to attend to your customer first – however, the key is explaining to your boss why you are needed urgently by the customer, and then to assure your boss that you will attend to his or her needs as soon as possible (unless it's absolutely an urgent matter).

77: What is the most important aspect of customer service?

Answer:

While many people would simply state that customer satisfaction is the most important aspect of customer service, it's important to be able to elaborate on other important techniques in customer service situations. Explain why customer service is such a key part of business, and be sure to expand on the aspect that you deem to be the most important in a way that is reasoned and well-thought out.

78: Is it best to create low or high expectations for a customer?

Answer:

You may answer this question either way (after, of course, determining that the company does not have a clear opinion on the matter). However, no matter which way you answer the question, you must display a thorough thought process, and very clear reasoning for the option you chose. Offer pros and cons of each, and include the ultimate point that tips the scale in favor of your chosen answer.

And Finally Good Luck!

INDEX

JSP-Servlet Interview Questions

Servlet

23: How would you make servlet stop timing-out when processing a long database query?

24: Why is HttpServlet declared as abstract even though it has concrete methods?

25: How would you refresh a servlet automatically if any data gets updated into database?

26: Describe the difference between URL encoding and URL rewriting.

27: What is the use of Servlet Wrapper classes?

28: What is servlet chaining?

29: What are the functions of the Servlet Container?

30: What is Server Side push and what is it used for?

31: What is Client refresh/Client pull mechanism and how do we achieve it?

32: How would you achieve/make Client Auto Refresh using servlets?

33: What types of protocols are supported by HttpServlet?

34: How would you send data from servlet to Javascript?

35: How would you retrieve the name and version number of servlet or JSP engine?

36: What is meant by parsequerystring?

37: Which one is better to write binary data: JSP or servlet?

Servlet Lifecycle

38: You have a counter to know how many times your webpage was accessed. Where will you initialize it and where will you increment the counter? Explain.

39: Explain what happens during the initialization stage of a servlet.

40: How do you pass hidden values from the form to the server?

41: You request a servlet and it fails midway, what happens to initialized objects, variables and loaded classes?

42: Can we replace the servlet init() method with a constructor?

43: If 10 users access a login page of your application at the same time,

Servlet Reloading / Loading

63: What will happen if a servlet is not loaded into the memory but the client had requested that servlet?

64: What is lazy loading in servlet?

65: Is there any way to unload a servlet from a web server memory without restarting the server?

66: What is the reason of disabling auto reloading feature in production environment?

Servlet Context

67: How do you add web components in Servlet 3 dynamically?

68: Differentiate between Servlet Context and Page Context.

69: What are the uses of ServletContext?

70: When is a servlet listener preferred over servlet context?

71: Can I access the ServletContext in one servlet from another servlet? Explain.

72: What is the difference between <context-param> and <init-param> given in web.xml?

73: What is the difference between ServletConfig and ServletContext interfaces?

74: When is the ServletContext object created?

75: What is ServletContext object?

76: How many contexts will be created if five applications are running in a web container?

77: Can we access ServletContext parameters in the JSP page and how would you retrieve it?

78: How would you make a ServletContext object thread safe?

79: How do you retrieve the servlet context?

80: What is the use of servletcontext method and getResourceAsStream()?

81: How do you avoid hard coding the database name and driver details in all the servlets?

Session Management

browser has disabled the cookies?

105: What is the maximum cookie size and how many cookies we can store in response object?

106: How would you set inactivity lease period on a per-session basis?

107: What are the ways to destroy a session?

108: Which session tracking mechanism does not have a size limit and which has good performance?

109: What is the use of setSecure() and getSecure() methods in Cookies ?

110: How would you prevent a JSP page from creating a session automatically?

111: What is the use of setComment() and getComment() methods in Cookies?

Session Object

112: What are the differences between cookies and sessions?

113: Why should we create our own cookies instead of using the browser cookies?

114: How can you make the session persistent?

115: What are the real-time circumstances when the session ends?

116: How do you implement single sign-on for multiple applications?

117: How will you store and retrieve your form data into session objects?

118: You would like to update your account profile details. Where should you enter your username and profile password again? How should we verify if this username is the same as the logged in username?

119: What is the default Session status in a JSP page and how can it be changed?

120: Request object will not be used to pass data from JSP to servlet. Then how can we achieve it?

121: Is there any size limitation for the data which is stored in a session object?

122: How would you know if the http session is removed (when time

Servlet Event Listeners

141: What are the different types of Event Listeners available for handling Session level events?

142: How would you access the session if you use event handling listener interfaces?

143: A class implements HttpSessionBindingListener and its object is stored in session. If the session is invalidated what will happen?

Servlet Filter

144: What is a ServletFilter and what is it used for?

145: What is the difference between a Servlet and a Filter?

146: What are Filter lifecycle methods?

147: Explain the ServletFilter lifecyle.

148: How to transfer control from one filter to another?

149: What are the interfaces available in ServletFilter?

150: What is FilterChain?

151: How would you access the ServletContext parameter in your filter init() method?

152: How would the servlet container invoke the filters?

JSP and Servlet

153: What is the difference between JSP and a servlet?

154: Why would you require calling a JSP page from servlet?

155: How would you make a JSP generated servlet subclass the custom servlet class instead of using the default one?

156: If JSP page "login.jsp" contains an instance variable as "String name" and the "chgPwd.jsp" file also contains an instance variable as "String name". What will happen if the client requests login.jsp?

157: What is the use of inter-servlet communication?

158: How do we use JDB logger in a JSP page?

159: Describe the difference between 2-tier and 3-tier architecture.

JSP Lifecycle and Methods

JSP Implicit Object

JSP Tags

178: Can we declare methods within a JSPDeclaration tag?

179: What is the use of <jsp:fallback> tag?

180: What is the nature of the variables declared in the Scriptlet tags and Declaration tags?

181: How would you declare variables within the Scriptlet and Declaration tags? Explain with an example.

182: What is the difference between JSP and HTML comments?

183: How would you invoke a servlet from JSPor from another JSP?

184: What are custom tags?

185: How does the JSP engines instantiate tag handler class instances?

JSP Actions

186: What is the difference between JSP include action and include directive? What are they used for?

187: What are the different actions available in JSP?

188: When would JSP Actions and JSP Directives be processed?

189: What are the scopes available for <jsp:usebean>?

190: How would you provide/pass data from the main JSP to an included JSP?

191: Can we set value of page attribute in <jsp:include> ?

192: How would you pass values while forwarding control from one JSP to another JSP/servlet?

193: How would you generate an XML file from a JSP page?

194: How would you use JavaBeans in JSP page?

195: What will happen if you don't select the correct scope in the<jsp:useBean> tag?

196: How would you pass information from one/main JSP to included JSP?

getParameter()

197: How will you retrieve the JSP form data into your JSP file?

Response Object

PrintWriter, JspWriter

Miscellaneous

216: What are the different types of directives available in JSP?

217: Explain Page directives in JSP.

218: When do you use include directive and include action in JSP?

219: What is the default option of the session attribute in page directive and which is more efficient?

220: How do we handle caching in a JSP page?

221: What are the differences between Application server and Webserver?

222: How would you inform the browser not to cache the pages?

223: How would you implement caching in JSP?

224: What are the caching mechanisms available for a JSP page to improve the performance?

225: Explain the various caching techniques available for JSP.

226: How will you redirect one JSP to another resource (JSP/servlet)?

227: What is the difference between <jsp:forward> and response.sendRedirect()?

228: What is the main difference between SendRedirect and RequestDispatcher?

229: Can we write database connection/jdbc code in JSP?

230: In which of the servlet's lifecycle method would you prefer to create a database connection?

231: How would you create connections for many users?

232: If you are retrieving data from a database and the result set have null values, how would the values be printed in the JSP input text fields?

233: If you set a request attribute in the JSP, will it be accessible in the subsequent servlet code?

234: Can we set values for the parameters of the included JSP (jsp2) in the main JSP(jsp1).

235: How would you pass information using request object from a servlet and forward it to a JSP? (or) explain how does a servlet communicate with a JSPpage?

258: How would you configure servlet authentication in web.xml?

259: How would you send user authentication information while creating a URL connection?

260: How would you send a file to a browser from your application or download a file from the application?

261: How would you send a file from the browser to application or upload a file to your application?

262: What are the considerations for Servlet Clustering?

263: What is the difference between encodeURL and encodeRedirectURL?

264: What is URL Encoding and URL Decoding?

265: How would you know if the http session is removed (when time outs)?

266: How do we set query and database driver details in JSP using JSTL?

267: What is internationalization (I18N) and locale?

268: How would you detect Locale in a JSP page?

269: Describe EL and what it can be used for.

270: In which order does EL search for an attribute?

271: How would you disable EL in JSP?

272: What implicit EL objects are available in JSP?

273: Why do we need a thread pool for the JSP engine?

274: What do you mean by Connection Pooling?

275: Can we use ServletOutputStream object from JSP?

276: What is the use of <load-on-startup> tag in web.xml?

277: What is a deployment descriptor?

278: How will you retrieve the multiple init parameters of a servlet defined in web.xml?

279: The remote server details such as name and IP are given in <init-param> tag (web.xml) and the connection is being done in a servlet called ConnServlet.java. If I move all the data to another server, what are the changes that need to be done?

280: Explain session migration.

HR Questions

20: Tell me about a time when you discovered something in the workplace that was disrupting your (or others) productivity – what did you do about it?

21: How do you perform in a job with clearly-defined objectives and goals?

22: How do you perform in a job where you have great decision-making power?

23: If you saw another employee doing something dishonest or unethical, what would you do?

24: Tell me about a time when you learned something on your own that later helped in your professional life.

25: Tell me about a time when you developed a project idea at work.

26: Tell me about a time when you took a risk on a project.

27: What would you tell someone who was looking to get into this field?

28: Tell me about a time when you worked additional hours to finish a project.

29: Tell me about a time when your performance exceeded the duties and requirements of your job.

30: What is your driving attitude about work?

31: Do you take work home with you?

32: Describe a typical work day to me.

33: Tell me about a time when you went out of your way at your previous job.

34: Are you open to receiving feedback and criticisms on your job performance, and adjusting as necessary?

35: What inspires you?

36: How do you inspire others?

37: How do you make decisions?

38: What are the most difficult decisions for you to make?

39: When making a tough decision, how do you gather information?

40: Tell me about a decision you made that did not turn out well.

2008 elections?

66: Explain X task in a few short sentences as you would to a second-grader.

67: If you could compare yourself to any animal, what would it be?

68: Who is your hero?

69: Who would play you in the movie about your life?

70: Name five people, alive or dead, that would be at your ideal dinner party.

71: What is customer service?

72: Tell me about a time when you went out of your way for a customer.

73: How do you gain confidence from customers?

74: Tell me about a time when a customer was upset or agitated – how did you handle the situation?

75: When can you make an exception for a customer?

76: What would you do in a situation where you were needed by both a customer and your boss?

77: What is the most important aspect of customer service?

78: Is it best to create low or high expectations for a customer?

Some of the following titles might also be handy:

1. .NET Interview Questions You'll Most Likely Be Asked
2. 200 Interview Questions You'll Most Likely Be Asked
3. Access VBA Programming Interview Questions You'll Most Likely Be Asked
4. Adobe ColdFusion Interview Questions You'll Most Likely Be Asked
5. Advanced Excel Interview Questions You'll Most Likely Be Asked
6. Advanced JAVA Interview Questions You'll Most Likely Be Asked
7. Advanced SAS Interview Questions You'll Most Likely Be Asked
8. AJAX Interview Questions You'll Most Likely Be Asked
9. Algorithms Interview Questions You'll Most Likely Be Asked
10. Android Development Interview Questions You'll Most Likely Be Asked
11. Ant & Maven Interview Questions You'll Most Likely Be Asked
12. Apache Web Server Interview Questions You'll Most Likely Be Asked
13. Artificial Intelligence Interview Questions You'll Most Likely Be Asked
14. ASP.NET Interview Questions You'll Most Likely Be Asked
15. Automated Software Testing Interview Questions You'll Most Likely Be Asked
16. Base SAS Interview Questions You'll Most Likely Be Asked
17. BEA WebLogic Server Interview Questions You'll Most Likely Be Asked
18. C & C++ Interview Questions You'll Most Likely Be Asked
19. C# Interview Questions You'll Most Likely Be Asked
20. C++ Internals Interview Questions You'll Most Likely Be Asked
21. CCNA Interview Questions You'll Most Likely Be Asked
22. Cloud Computing Interview Questions You'll Most Likely Be Asked
23. Computer Architecture Interview Questions You'll Most Likely Be Asked
24. Computer Networks Interview Questions You'll Most Likely Be Asked
25. Core JAVA Interview Questions You'll Most Likely Be Asked
26. Data Structures & Algorithms Interview Questions You'll Most Likely Be Asked
27. Data WareHousing Interview Questions You'll Most Likely Be Asked
28. EJB 3.0 Interview Questions You'll Most Likely Be Asked
29. Entity Framework Interview Questions You'll Most Likely Be Asked
30. Fedora & RHEL Interview Questions You'll Most Likely Be Asked
31. GNU Development Interview Questions You'll Most Likely Be Asked
32. Hibernate, Spring & Struts Interview Questions You'll Most Likely Be Asked
33. HTML, XHTML and CSS Interview Questions You'll Most Likely Be Asked
34. HTML5 Interview Questions You'll Most Likely Be Asked
35. IBM WebSphere Application Server Interview Questions You'll Most Likely Be Asked
36. iOS SDK Interview Questions You'll Most Likely Be Asked
37. Java / J2EE Design Patterns Interview Questions You'll Most Likely Be Asked
38. Java / J2EE Interview Questions You'll Most Likely Be Asked
39. Java Messaging Service Interview Questions You'll Most Likely Be Asked
40. JavaScript Interview Questions You'll Most Likely Be Asked
41. JavaServer Faces Interview Questions You'll Most Likely Be Asked
42. JDBC Interview Questions You'll Most Likely Be Asked
43. jQuery Interview Questions You'll Most Likely Be Asked
44. JSP-Servlet Interview Questions You'll Most Likely Be Asked
45. JUnit Interview Questions You'll Most Likely Be Asked
46. Linux Commands Interview Questions You'll Most Likely Be Asked
47. Linux Interview Questions You'll Most Likely Be Asked
48. Linux System Administrator Interview Questions You'll Most Likely Be Asked
49. Mac OS X Lion Interview Questions You'll Most Likely Be Asked
50. Mac OS X Snow Leopard Interview Questions You'll Most Likely Be Asked

51. Microsoft Access Interview Questions You'll Most Likely Be Asked
52. Microsoft Excel Interview Questions You'll Most Likely Be Asked
53. Microsoft Powerpoint Interview Questions You'll Most Likely Be Asked
54. Microsoft Word Interview Questions You'll Most Likely Be Asked
55. MySQL Interview Questions You'll Most Likely Be Asked
56. NetSuite Interview Questions You'll Most Likely Be Asked
57. Networking Interview Questions You'll Most Likely Be Asked
58. OOPS Interview Questions You'll Most Likely Be Asked
59. Operating Systems Interview Questions You'll Most Likely Be Asked
60. Oracle DBA Interview Questions You'll Most Likely Be Asked
61. Oracle E-Business Suite Interview Questions You'll Most Likely Be Asked
62. ORACLE PL/SQL Interview Questions You'll Most Likely Be Asked
63. Perl Programming Interview Questions You'll Most Likely Be Asked
64. PHP Interview Questions You'll Most Likely Be Asked
65. PMP Interview Questions You'll Most Likely Be Asked
66. Python Interview Questions You'll Most Likely Be Asked
67. RESTful JAVA Web Services Interview Questions You'll Most Likely Be Asked
68. Ruby Interview Questions You'll Most Likely Be Asked
69. Ruby on Rails Interview Questions You'll Most Likely Be Asked
70. SAP ABAP Interview Questions You'll Most Likely Be Asked
71. SAP HANA Interview Questions You'll Most Likely Be Asked
72. SAS Programming Guidelines Interview Questions You'll Most Likely Be Asked
73. Selenium Testing Tools Interview Questions You'll Most Likely Be Asked
74. Silverlight Interview Questions You'll Most Likely Be Asked
75. Software Repositories Interview Questions You'll Most Likely Be Asked
76. Software Testing Interview Questions You'll Most Likely Be Asked
77. SQL Server Interview Questions You'll Most Likely Be Asked
78. Tomcat Interview Questions You'll Most Likely Be Asked
79. UML Interview Questions You'll Most Likely Be Asked
80. Unix Interview Questions You'll Most Likely Be Asked
81. UNIX Shell Programming Interview Questions You'll Most Likely Be Asked
82. VB.NET Interview Questions You'll Most Likely Be Asked
83. Windows Server 2008 R2 Interview Questions You'll Most Likely Be Asked
84. XLXP, XSLT, XPATH, XFORMS & XQuery Interview Questions You'll Most Likely Be Asked
85. XML Interview Questions You'll Most Likely Be Asked

www.ingramcontent.com/pod-product-compliance
Lightning Source LLC
Chambersburg PA
CBHW061248220326
41599CB00028B/5577

* 9 7 8 1 9 4 6 3 8 3 1 0 5 *